RAND ARROYO CENTER

T0302568

Enhancing Critical Thinking Skills for Army Leaders Using Blended-Learning Methods

Susan G. Straus, Michael G. Shanley, Maria C. Lytell, James C. Crowley, Sara H. Bana, Megan Clifford, Kristin J. Leuschner

Prepared for the United States Army

Approved for public release; distribution unlimited

The research described in this report was sponsored by the United States Army under Contract No. W74V8H-06-C-0001.

Library of Congress Cataloging-in-Publication Data

Straus, Susan G.
Enhancing critical thinking skills for Army leaders using blended-learning methods / Susan G. Straus, Michael G. Shanley, Maria C. Lytell, James C. Crowley, Sarah H. Bana, Megan Clifford, Kristin J. Leuschner.
pages cm
Includes bibliographical references.
ISBN 978-0-8330-7909-1 (pbk. : alk. paper)
1. Military education—Technological innovations—United States. 2. United States. Army—Officers—Training of. 3. Blended learning—United States. 4. Distance education—United States—Computer-assisted instruction. I. Title.

U408.3.S84 2013
355.5'5—dc23

2013025049

The RAND Corporation is a nonprofit institution that helps improve policy and decisionmaking through research and analysis. RAND's publications do not necessarily reflect the opinions of its research clients and sponsors.

Support RAND—make a tax-deductible charitable contribution at www.rand.org/giving/contribute.html

RAND® is a registered trademark

© Copyright 2013 RAND Corporation

This document and trademark(s) contained herein are protected by law. This representation of RAND intellectual property is provided for noncommercial use only. Unauthorized posting of RAND documents to a non-RAND website is prohibited. RAND documents are protected under copyright law. Permission is given to duplicate this document for personal use only, as long as it is unaltered and complete. Permission is required from RAND to reproduce, or reuse in another form, any of our research documents for commercial use. For information on reprint and linking permissions, please see the RAND permissions page (www.rand.org/pubs/permissions.html).

RAND OFFICES

SANTA MONICA, CA • WASHINGTON, DC

PITTSBURGH, PA • NEW ORLEANS, LA • JACKSON, MS • BOSTON, MA

DOHA, QA • CAMBRIDGE, UK • BRUSSELS, BE

www.rand.org

Preface

In this project, "Enhancing Distributed Learning for Leader Education Through Blended-Learning Methods and Technologies," the U.S. Army Training and Doctrine Command asked RAND Arroyo Center to support the Army's efforts to improve the distributed delivery of Intermediate Level Education (ILE) by examining the potential of various blended learning methods and technologies and by identifying directions to improve the Advanced Operations Course and related courses.

This report describes a set of studies designed to evaluate the ILE Advanced Operations Course taught via blended distributed learning and to identify areas for improvement in course design and delivery. The report also discusses evaluation approaches to support continuous improvement in ILE. The report will be of interest to those involved in planning, developing, delivering, and evaluating leader education and those who develop and implement distributed learning courses that incorporate group collaboration on topics involving complex analytical skills and related competencies.

This research was sponsored by U.S. Army Training and Doctrine Command and was conducted within RAND Arroyo Center's Manpower and Training Program. RAND Arroyo Center, part of the RAND Corporation, is a federally funded research and development center sponsored by the United States Army.

The Project Unique Identification Code (PUIC) for the project that produced this document is RAN126140.

For more information on RAND Arroyo Center, contact the Director of Operations (telephone 310-393-0411, extension 6419; fax 310-451-6952; email Marcy_Agmon@rand.org), or visit Arroyo's website at http://www.rand.org/ard.html.

Contents

Figures

Tables

Summary

As the Army looks for more cost-effective, relevant, and timely means of delivering education and training, it has increasingly turned to distributed learning. Historically, technology-based distributed learning consisted largely of single-learner, self-paced interactive multimedia instruction. However, such methods may not be effective for all types of training and education, particularly those that involve teamwork; group communication; critical thinking; and joint, interagency, intergovernmental, and multinational operations. The Command and General Staff School's (CGSS's) Advanced Operations Course (AOC) is one example of a leader professional development course focused on Army Learning Model competencies. AOC focuses on developing junior field-grade staff officers' skills, including the wide range of complex cognitive skills involved in planning military operations, with students working collaboratively as members of an operational and tactical level staff. It is the second phase of Intermediate Level Education (ILE), building on the Common Core course.

CGSS offers AOC using both a traditional resident model and a model that the school refers to as *blended distributed learning* (BDL). AOC-BDL requires substantial instructor-student and student-student interaction but is completely distributed. That is, the course uses a computer-supported cooperative learning (CSCL) model with extensive synchronous and asynchronous collaboration among students and instructors, who are distributed geographically and across time zones. When charged with providing AOC to all Army branch officers in all regions of the world without affecting the personnel operating tempo, CGSS adopted a BDL model as a flexible approach to achieve throughput and meet course goals. However, relatively little is known about the effectiveness of using a completely distributed approach to support the acquisition of critical thinking skills and related competencies.

The purpose of the study was to build on prior RAND Arroyo Center research on the effectiveness of the delivery venues for the ILE Common Core by examining outcomes for AOC-BDL. This study had three objectives: to assess AOC-BDL effectiveness, to identify best practices in CSCL, and to use findings from these efforts to identify options for improving AOC-BDL. To conduct the study, we analyzed responses to exit surveys measuring student satisfaction and perceptions of course quality and impact and piloted a survey of former graduates who completed the 2009–2010 AOC curriculum sometime in the past two years. We also conducted a review of research literature on blended learning and conducted original case studies of blended learning programs in civilian higher education, military education, and industry.

We adapted Benbunan-Fich, Hiltz, and Harasim's (2005) online interaction learning model (see Figure S.1) as a conceptual framework for this study. Benbunan-Fich et al. posited that *input factors*, such as technology and course characteristics, influence *learning processes*, which in turn affect *outcomes*, such as learning and satisfaction.

The main components of the framework are as follows:

- **Inputs**: These comprise all the resources (including people) and contextual factors that contribute to the learning experience, including characteristics of technology, the course, instructors, students, and the organizational context.
- **Learning processes**: These are the ways through which people learn, e.g., the types and extent of interactions between students and course content, instructors, and other students (Moore, 1989).
- **Outcomes**: The framework includes the outcomes shown in Figure S.1 (learning effectiveness, scale or cost-effectiveness, access, student satisfaction, and faculty satisfaction). In this study, we focused primarily on two factors: learning effectiveness (as perceived by the students) and student satisfaction.

Figure S.1
Framework for Online Learning

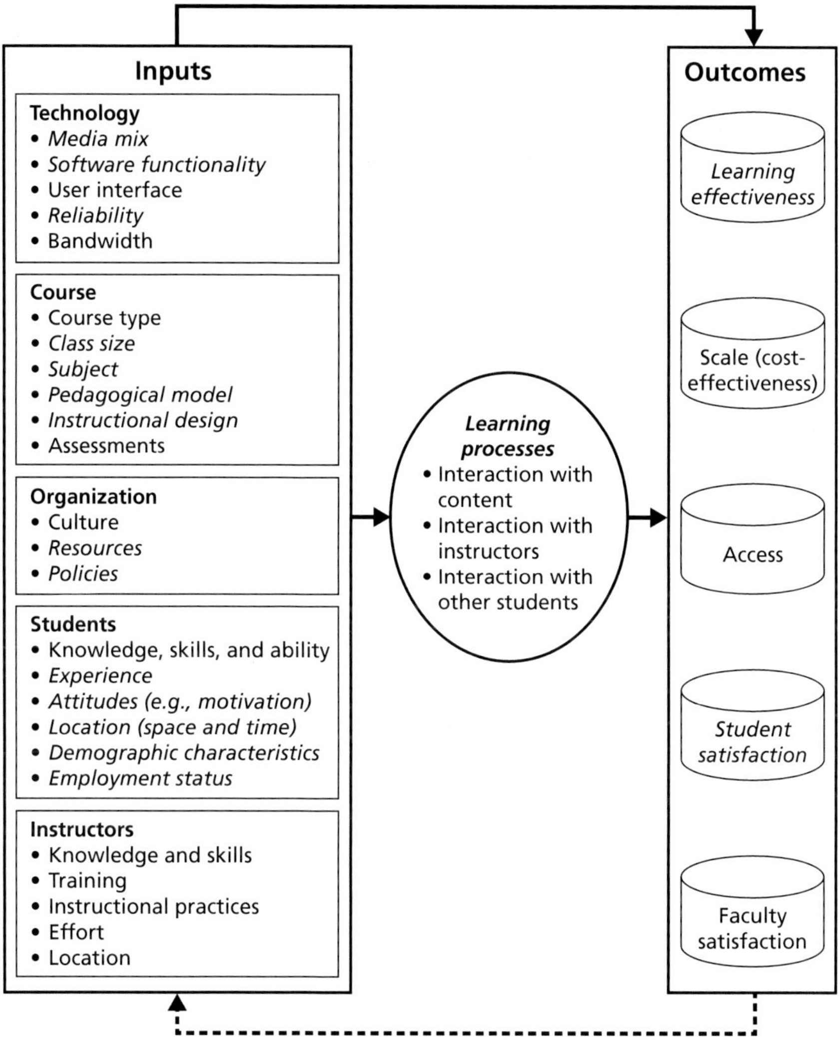

SOURCE: Adapted from Benbunan-Fich, Hiltz, and Harasim, 2005.
NOTE: Items in italics are addressed in this report.
RAND *RR172-A-S.1*

The Blended Distributed Learning Advanced Operations Course

AOC-BDL was modeled after residential AOC, and the two venues are intended to be equivalent. Several course input factors are central to our analysis, conclusions, and suggested options for improvement in course design and delivery. These include the following:

- **Students.** The course includes students from both the active component and the reserve component (RC). Most students work full time and have families. Students typically complete the course requirements in addition to their normal work or duty day requirements and on weekends; therefore, they have many competing demands on their own time.
- **Course content and structure.** The course involves complex subject matter across multiple echelons and emphasizes peer collaboration and development of staff products. AOC develops the officer's abilities to analyze complex problems and recommend potential solutions and to build and ethically lead operational and tactical formations in a joint environment, among other goals. It has the equivalent of the 308 traditional classroom hours of instruction. To support a collaborative approach, AOC students are organized into 16-person groups called "staff groups," each of which is composed of officers representing as broad a mix of branches and operational experience as possible. Although some of the course content is completed individually, using interactive multimedia instruction (IMI), readings, and written assignments, a significant portion of the course uses virtual synchronous activities, including online classroom sessions (up to 20, two-hour sessions), and collaboration among students, to develop the staff products. Students are also required to participate in online threaded discussions about course topics.
- **Instructional technology.** A range of technologies supports synchronous and asynchronous instruction, including Blackboard's learning management system; Defense Connect Online (DCO), which is used for online synchronous interaction; IMI, also

referred to as computer-based instruction; simulations; and other communication media, such as email and telephone. Technologies that are supported by CGSS run in a "dotmil" domain.
- **Policy.** Department of the Army policy requires completion of the Common Core and AOC for promotion to lieutenant colonel in the active component and for promotion to colonel in the RC. Completion of both courses may also increase RC officers' potential for selection to many career-enhancing assignments. Unlike their colleagues in the resident course, students are not formally provided paid duty time to take AOC-BDL, and commanders are not required to allow students to take the course on duty time. Most students in this study reported working on discretionary time.

Satisfaction and Perceived Learning Effectiveness in AOC-BDL

In this section, we describe findings from a student survey administered at the end of AOC ("exit survey") and the results of a pilot survey given to former AOC-BDL graduates ("postgraduate survey").

Students Were Generally Satisfied with the Course

Responses to the exit survey indicate that nearly 80 percent of students felt that AOC-BDL achieved its core purpose. Most students gave favorable ratings to learning effectiveness for computer-based instruction and to operational topics, such as understanding joint force capabilities and limitations, the joint operational planning process, and change management processes. Most students also reported that they were satisfied with aspects of the learning environment, such as instruction quality and peer interaction and feedback, and they were generally satisfied with the course overall.

However, 50 percent of students in the exit survey and 29 percent of students in the postgraduate survey reported that they would not recommend the course to others. Although we do not have conclusive evidence about the reasons for these responses, some possible alternatives are addressed next.

Students Noted Problems with Computer-Supported Collaboration for Learning

Students provided many detailed responses to open-ended questions about course design and delivery. A common theme in these comments, not reflected in other survey questions, pertained to issues with computer-supported collaboration and learning. As shown in Figure S.2, the preponderance of comments focused on the CSCL approach. While some comments were positive, the majority were negative. A number of students felt that face-to-face interaction was needed, particularly for such topics as the military decision making process (MDMP); the most common recommendation was to have a one- to two-week in-person exercise at the end of the course.

Students' Ratings of Course Effectiveness Suggest Improvement May Be Needed for Instruction of Some Course Topics

While students were satisfied with instruction for some operational topics, as described above, their ratings may indicate needs for improvement in general critical field-grade competencies. Among former graduates, approximately 40 to 60 percent reported small or no improvement in conducting MDMP, complex problem solving, organizational leadership, and oral and written communication (see Figure S.3). In addition, although most reported that the course prepared them to lead in Army and joint environments, students felt less prepared for operations in the international and interagency domains.

Some Students Emphasized that the Completely Distributed Environment Posed Challenges to Meeting Course Goals

Figure S.4 shows the negative sentiments about specific aspects of the CSCL approach. Most comments emphasized that the completely distributed environment impeded some course learning goals, such as

Figure S.2
Frequencies of Positive and Negative Comments—Exit Survey

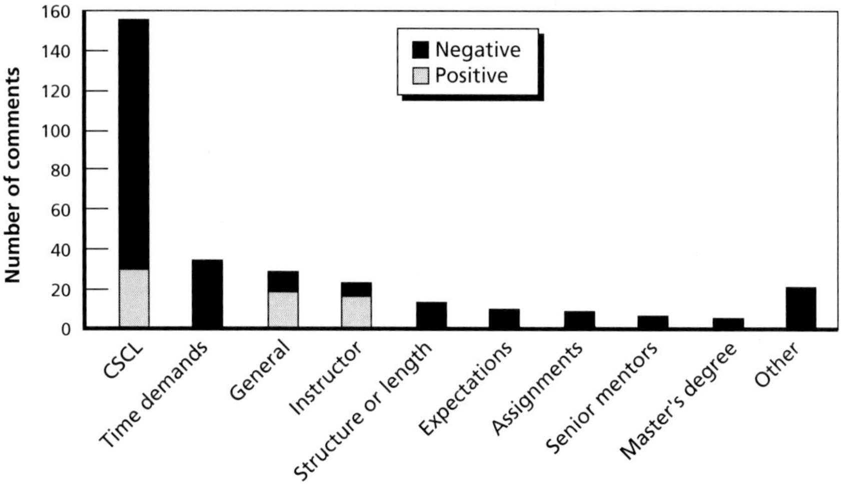

RAND *RR172-A-S.2*

Figure S.3
Postgraduate Achievement of Critical Field-Grade Competencies

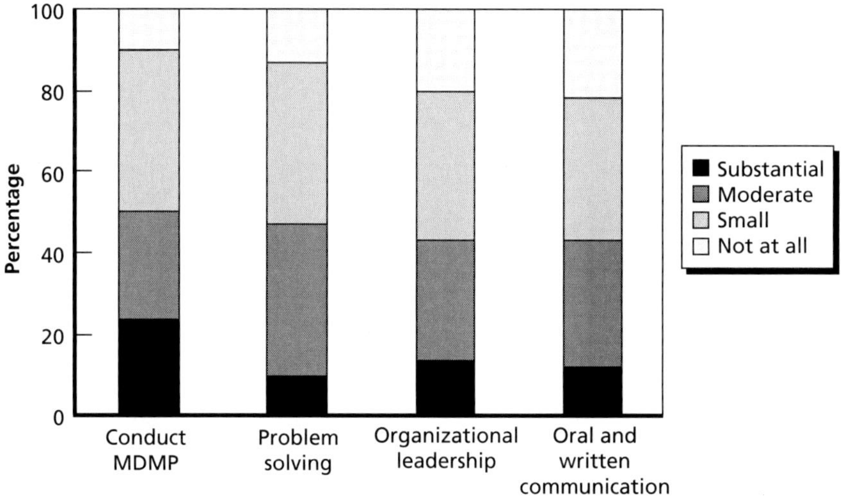

RAND *RR172-A-S.3*

MDMP. Students also cited a variety of challenges to group coordination in terms of technology reliability and access, competing demands on their time, complexity of the coursework, and the challenges of working across time zones. Likewise, a number of the respondents in the postgraduate survey commented that face-to-face interaction was needed for truly effective learning and that, while the available technologies could support collaboration, conducting the MDMP process online was not beneficial. Although respondents reported being satisfied with peer feedback, students in both surveys noted other problems with collaboration, such as free riding (members not pulling their weight) and difficulties scheduling synchronous sessions with their teams.

The Reliability of Technology Posed Problems for Some Students

Approximately 30 to 40 percent of former graduates reported one or more problems with issues such as technical difficulties with computer-based instruction or reliable computer/Internet access. Not surpris-

Figure S.4
Specific Categories of Negative Comments About CSCL—Exit Survey

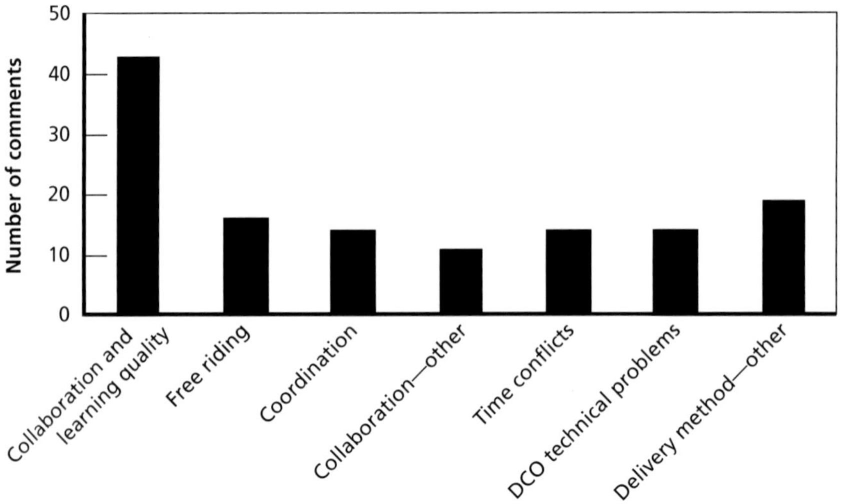

RAND *RR172-A-S.4*

ingly, technical issues, such as Internet access, were more problematic among students who were located outside the continental United States during part or all of the course. Similar questions in the exit survey showed that 13 to 23 percent of respondents had trouble accessing a reliable computer; playing audio, video, or animations; or accessing the course over the Internet. CGSS staff confirmed that technical problems with DCO and Blackboard were common.

Student Characteristics May Constrain Participation or Engagement in AOC-BDL

Several characteristics of the student population present obstacles to working on the course. Students reported substantial work and family commitments and responded that these responsibilities interfered with working on the course (or that working on the course was a distraction to performing their jobs). Only 14 percent of graduates reported that work or family commitments *did not* interfere with working on the course.

Peer Collaboration, Interaction with Instructor, and Student Motivation Most Strongly Associated with Course Outcomes

We conducted a series of analyses to examine associations among inputs, processes, and outcomes, where *outcomes* refers to overall satisfaction with the course and perceived learning effectiveness. There were several key findings. First, regarding input variables, whereas students' ratings of technology reliability were not associated with outcomes, work and family commitments were negatively associated with satisfaction (but not with learning effectiveness). Second, student motivation for taking the course was strongly associated with satisfaction and perceived learning effectiveness. Graduates who took AOC-BDL to improve their performance or professionalism were more satisfied and reported greater learning than those who took the course for promotion or another reason (e.g., to avoid moving or because they were told the course was required). Third, students' ratings of the quality of interaction with instructors and peers explained a substantial portion of outcome ratings beyond the effects of the input variables. Ratings of collaboration processes partially or fully mediated (accounted for) the effect of inputs on outcome ratings. For example, work and family commitments had a negative effect on collaborative learning processes, which in turn affected satisfaction. These results highlight the importance of collaborative processes in the course.

Literature Review and Case Studies of BDL

Both the literature review and case studies focused on blended learning and distributed blended learning for adult learners in courses that address topics relevant to AOC (e.g., complex skills, collaboration). The literature review focused on empirical research published from 2007–2012, as well as seminal articles published prior to 2007; it also examined studies of virtual team collaboration. Our original case studies included Pennsylvania State University's (PSU's) World Campus, which offers 80 degree or certificate programs; the Naval Postgraduate School (NPS), an accredited graduate-level education and research institution run by the U.S. Navy; and Xerox's Service Delivery eXcellence, which teaches executives and managers service delivery and ways to solve service-related problems for clients and to expand business opportunities. We supplemented these original case studies with findings from published cases.

No Clear Advantage for Resident Instruction or Blended Learning, But There Are Few Examples of Effective All-Distributed BDL

A number of studies have investigated the use of various instructional media for adult learners. Many of these studies compared resident instruction and distributed learning and, for the most part, found no clear advantage for one medium or the other. Some recent meta-analyses concluded that distributed learning has an advantage, but many of the studies included in these analyses have methodological weaknesses, such as selection biases. Moreover, there are few studies of effective all-distributed BDL.

However, we did find a few examples of BDL relevant to AOC, including the award-winning Service Delivery eXcellence program at Xerox, which teaches leadership skills to executives and managers around the globe; a pilot project to teach entrepreneurship education at three Canadian universities (Bisson et al., 2005); and a field experiment comparing face-to-face and online courses for community psychologists in Italy (Francescato et al., 2007). All three examples document successful delivery of BDL.

Instructional Design, Not Venue, Is Key Determinant of Effectiveness

Learning programs are effective when instructional strategies are designed to be compatible with human learning processes (Clark and Mayer, 2011). Thus, good instructional design will often differ according to the delivery medium used. Residential and distributed learning designs can differ along many dimensions, including instructional approach, collaborative practices, feedback mechanisms, and grading strategies.

Although scholars have concluded that blended learning and residential learning require different instructional designs, many experts believe that effective blended learning dealing with complex material requires some degree of in-person instruction (e.g., Bernard et al., 2004). In fact, standard definitions of blended learning (which include some face-to-face instruction) and the scarcity of BDL programs and research may be indications of the perceived need for some in-person instructional activities, particularly when teaching such skills as leadership.

New Technologies and Instructional Modalities Require Support to Be Effectively Adopted for Complex Learning

Instructors are more likely to adopt a technology if they anticipate that it will be beneficial to student learning, if it is easy to use, and if they have institutional support for its use. Our case studies document how institutions can support technology following the recommendations of Park and Bonk (2007a), e.g., by providing professional development for online teaching and by having instructional designers and media specialists available to work with faculty on course development. In addition, our case studies revealed that commercial-off-the-shelf and open-source software for learning management systems and collaborative activities can successfully support BDL.

Successful Programs Find Ways to Reduce Conflicts with Students' Other Commitments

Like AOC-BDL students, many adult learners lead busy lives and are geographically dispersed. We found that successful programs find ways to reduce conflicts with students' other commitments. Programs use two general approaches to address time commitments and time-zone differences. First, they tend to limit the use of synchronous modalities, for example, by offering either distributed learning *or* blended learning with a residential segment, but not BDL. This was the option the PSU programs preferred; directors and staff members said that they continue to use distributed learning rather than move to BDL because their students would resist the restrictions on their time imposed by the need to participate in synchronous online sessions. A second approach is to engage students' employers to dedicate time for students' coursework. For example, NPS requires that organizations employing prospective students agree to give students dedicated time for the course.

Virtual and Collocated Groups Can Achieve Comparable Outcomes Under the Right Circumstances

Numerous studies comparing outcomes of collocated and virtual groups show that collocated groups perform better on interdependent tasks, such as decisionmaking and problem solving, and express more positive outcomes, such as cohesion and trust, in the short term. However, when time is not constrained or when virtual teams interact over time, virtual teams "catch up" to collocated teams in performance and social outcomes. Nonetheless, there are a variety of important processes in collocated teams that are difficult to replicate in distributed groups, and, as a result, virtual teams sometimes interact in ways that inhibit collaborative learning.

Successful Programs Use a Variety of Methods to Foster Student Engagement and Success in Virtual Interactive Activities

Case studies describe options instructors use to engage students and help them succeed in virtual collaboration activities. First, many instructors train students to ensure that they know how to use the technology. Second, instructors can "scaffold" discussions and provide timely feedback. For example, in the NPS Program Management master's program, instructors pose challenging questions in class or "cold call" on students to answer questions. Third, using small (rather than large) groups for interactive activities can alleviate free riding and facilitate interaction and coordination. Fourth, peer evaluations are used to increase accountability in teams.

Conclusions and Options for Improvement

AOC-BDL Has a Number of Strengths

In summary, AOC-BDL has a number of strengths. Despite significant constraints, most students report that AOC-BDL meets its core purpose. Furthermore, students give high ratings to items about the importance of student-instructor and student-student interaction, and students are consistently satisfied with their instructors. Students also report that most computer-based instruction lessons are effective. These indicators of success are more impressive in light of the fact that many students do not have a choice about the medium; that is, they cannot choose whether to attend the resident course or the BDL course. In contrast, educational institutions often give students a choice about enrolling in a resident or DL course; as a result, the relative effectiveness of these methods is often difficult to determine. CGSS's continuous improvement process is yet another strength in that it gives the school many opportunities to make needed adjustments to the course.

In addition to these strengths, participation in AOC-BDL provides some benefits that students in the resident course do not experience. Notably, by collaborating in virtual teams on complex tasks, students in AOC-BDL learn to work in situations that are increasingly common in operational environments and in other institutional settings.

Improvements Can Be Made

Despite these strengths, student responses indicate factors to consider in CGSS's continuous improvement process for AOC-BDL. Students' ratings of learning effectiveness suggest the need for further investigation of instruction of critical field-grade competencies and leadership in a range of operational environments. For example, it would be beneficial to obtain input from students' commanders before and after the course with respect to knowledge, skills, and abilities in these areas.

More important, changes are needed to foster better collaboration among students to facilitate learning and coordination. Currently, AOC-BDL has a number of input factors in conflict, including complex subject matter, requirements for collaboration at a distance, use of technologies that are time consuming for collaboration, and students who have limited time available to devote to the course. Options for improvement in course design and delivery focus on alleviating the tensions among these factors.

Improving Course Design and Delivery

We present a number of options for improvement in course design and delivery, summarized in Table S.1. These options are based on an integration of survey results with best practices identified in case studies and the research literature. Suggestions address input factors including course design, student characteristics, technology, and organizational policy.

Modify Course Design

Adding a resident segment to the class offers the greatest potential for improvement in learning processes and outcomes and is consistent with student recommendations and best practices in military and civilian higher education. However, this change is also the most complicated in terms of scheduling and resourcing. Indeed, this option may not be feasible because of available infrastructure, costs, and operational manning requirements associated with temporary duty and course staffing. In light of these constraints, we argue that the remaining strategies become particularly important to consider.

A second option is to shift some collaborative activities to higher-level IMI (e.g., Level 3) and have fewer but more in-depth synchronous exercises, with more time spent reviewing plans, discussing the rationale for students' decisions, and evaluating alternative courses of

Table S.1
Summary of Options to Improve Course Design and Delivery

Strategy	Suggestion
Course design	Add a 1- to 2-week resident period at the end of the course to work on the most intensive collaborative activities
	Shift some collaborative activities to higher-level IMI or other assignments with iterative student-instructor interaction; have fewer but more in-depth synchronous exercises
	Implement peer evaluations
	Offer additional instructor facilitation to student groups and train students in team facilitation skills
Composition of student groups	Use smaller groups for team assignments and for larger group exercises
	Compose groups based on time zone
Organizational policy	Encourage chain of command or employers to provide dedicated time for training
Technology	Move to a dotcom domain
	Pilot alternative technologies for group collaboration and group online gaming and simulations

action. This approach might free some instructional resources, but IMI can be costly to develop and maintain. Alternatively, students could be given complex analytic individual assignments with iterative student-instructor interaction to foster complex thinking skills.

To increase accountability, CGSS could implement peer evaluations that would contribute to course grades. Better facilitation for student groups as they work on their assignments (from instructors, or by training the students themselves to facilitate) could also reduce free riding. These options are low cost and could be executed in the near term.

Change Composition of Student Groups

Using smaller groups, such as eight-person rather than 16-person staff groups for some exercises, would reduce free riding and alleviate some of the coordination challenges that students reported. CGSS should emphasize to instructors the importance of composing groups based on time zone, and if a particular area of expertise needed for a group assignment is not available in a close time zone, providing a "stand-in" to serve in this role.

Affect Organizational Policy

It may be possible to reduce conflicts with job commitments by engaging students' employers (including commanders). This would entail finding ways to encourage commanders to provide duty time for required training. For RC students who work full time, CGSS could inform employers when an employee is taking the course, state expectations about what the student is required to do, and ask for support to allow the student to spend time on the course. Given that many of the skills addressed in AOC, such as problem solving, communication, and working in distributed teams, are relevant to a wide variety of jobs, the school might gain buy-in from employers by informing them how they can benefit from their employee's participation in the course.

Change Technology to Fit Course Design

Moving the course to a dotcom or dotedu domain could potentially alleviate some technology reliability issues that may inhibit access to the course. Hosting the course and tools for collaboration on a dotcom can also provide more options for collaborative technologies. For these reasons, Blackboard.com is being piloted with some staff groups, and CGSS anticipates moving to a dotcom domain entirely by 2014 (see Gould, 2013). A second suggestion is to continue to explore new technologies, including software for collaboration, as reported in our case studies, and technologies relevant to course content, such as online group games or simulations.

Expand Course Evaluation to Better Support a Continuous Improvement Process

Future evaluations of ILE courses should use a broader range of approaches. Although student assessments of their learning are often correlated with actual learning, survey responses are subjective. Future evaluations of AOC and other ILE courses should also analyze objective measures of learning, such as grades on assignments and tests. Because many of the competencies addressed in AOC are abstract, it may be helpful to provide information to students to demonstrate their knowledge gain use a pretest-posttest approach.

It is important to note that the exit and postgraduate surveys were administered only to students who completed the course. In the future, CGSS should also assess the perceptions of those who drop out and their reasons for attrition. This omission is a key gap, given that the attrition rate is currently estimated at 25 percent. As a result of that high rate, survey responses likely overestimate the satisfaction and perceived learning effectiveness of the course. More important, the attrition rate significantly increases the cost of the course per graduate and keeps waiting lists unnecessarily long. Assessing reasons for attrition in more depth could lend additional urgency to the changes already suggested in this report or could lead to additional improvements in the course that could reduce the dropout rate.

Using multiple methods and data sources is important to provide information about different aspects of the course. Other sources of data for evaluation include

- data from commanders regarding graduates' job performance following AOC completion
- interviews or focus groups with students or faculty to obtain detailed feedback about the learning experience and recommendations for improvement
- Web-based analytics to investigate student use of online materials
- independent subject-matter experts' observation of class sessions.

Concluding Thoughts

This study identified important options to consider when training complex material using group collaboration that is entirely distributed. Because AOC-BDL objectives and instructional methods support Army Learning Model goals and because the course has many positive features, this blended learning approach should be considered for other courses. However, alternative approaches to collaboration are needed when course activities involve collaboration on complex material. CGSS's experience and continuous development and evaluation efforts put the school in a position to identify such improvements and inform the Army training community about use of BDL for education and training.

Acknowledgments

This project would not have been possible without the assistance of many people in the Command and General Staff School. We especially wish to thank Daniel Ward for his support and contributions to this project. We are grateful for the expertise, time, and effort from Michael Martinez, Boyd Plessl, Patrick Cook, and Rick Steele. We also would like to acknowledge other AOC instructors who provided information and access to their course sessions.

We wish to acknowledge all the individuals who generously offered their time and expertise to make our case studies successful. Our many thanks to Thomas Mastre, Director of Educational Design, Development, and Distribution at NPS, for giving hours of his time to organize and host our visit. We are also very grateful to Wayne Smutz, Associate Vice President for Outreach and Executive Director of the World Campus at PSU, for speaking with us and providing access to his staff for interviews. However, our PSU case study would not have been complete without the assistance of two individuals: Alfred Turgeon, Emeritus, who served as our initial liaison to the World Campus, and Lawrence Ragan, Director of Instructional Design and Development and Director of Continuing and Distance Education/World Campus, who helped to identify PSU faculty members for interviews. We also wish to acknowledge the faculty members at NPS and PSU and program management at Xerox who spoke to us about their courses and programs. Finally, we wish to thank Bryan Chapman of Chapman Alliance for helping to identify and connect us to Xerox program management.

Many thanks to Charles Goldman at RAND and Robert Wisher for their detailed reviews on an earlier version of this report. We also wish to thank our RAND colleague, Michael Hansen, for his many contributions to this project.

Abbreviations

AC	active component
ADL	advanced distributed learning
AOC	Advanced Operations Course
AY	academic year
BDL	blended distributed learning
BL	blended learning
CBI	computer-based instruction
CGSC	Command and General Staff College
CGSOC	Command and General Staff Officer Course
CGSS	Command and General Staff School
CONUS	continental United States
CSCL	computer-supported cooperative learning
DCO	Defense Connect Online
DDE	Department of Distance Education
DL	distributed learning
DoD	Department of Defense
ICT	information and communication technology

ILE	Intermediate Level Education
IMI	interactive multimedia instruction
LMS	learning management system
MBA	Master of Business Administration
MDMP	military decision making process
NPS	Naval Postgraduate School
OCONUS	outside the continental United States
OPORD	operational order
PCS	permanent change of station
PSU	Pennsylvania State University
RC	reserve component
RL	residential learning
SDX	Service Delivery eXcellence
SME	subject matter expert
TASS	The Army School System
TCS	temporary change of station
TDY	temporary duty

CHAPTER ONE

Introduction

As the Army looks for more cost-effective, relevant, and timely means of delivering education and training, it has increasingly turned to distributed learning (DL), which typically uses a variety of technology-based methods, including Web-based approaches, to allow students to complete coursework at a distance. Historically, technology-based DL consisted largely of single-learner, self-paced interactive multimedia instruction (IMI). However, such methods may not be effective for all types of training and education, particularly those that involve teamwork; group communication; critical thinking; joint, interagency, intergovernmental, and multinational operations; and other competencies reflected in the Army Learning Model (U.S. Army Training and Doctrine Command, 2011).

The Command and General Staff School's (CGSS's) Advanced Operations Course (AOC) is one example of a leader professional development course focused on Army Learning Model competencies.[1] AOC develops junior field-grade staff officers' skills and provides commanders with the ability to build and lead operational staffs and tactical formations. It is the second phase of ILE, building on the Common Core course and a branch or functional specialty qualification course

[1] AOC is one phase of Intermediate Level Education (ILE), which focuses on education for Army majors. Prior to ILE, officers take Primary Level Education, which consists of the Basic Officer Leader Course for second lieutenants and the Captains Career Course. The Pre-Command Course for lieutenant colonels and Senior Level Education for colonels complete the professional military education sequence. Note that, subsequent to this research, the college renamed the ILE course to Command General Staff Officer Course (CGSOC).

that is based on the officer's career path.[2] Completion of this sequence is required for promotion to lieutenant colonel for officers in the active component (AC) and for promotion to colonel in the reserve component (RC).[3]

The Common Core curriculum consists of nine blocks (topic areas) of instruction. Six of these blocks address operational topics, such as Army and joint military strategy, capabilities, and operations. Three cross-cutting blocks (force management, history, and leadership) are supporting topics. The Common Core is taught in multiple venues: resident instruction at Fort Leavenworth; resident instruction in satellite locations; advanced distributed learning (ADL), which uses an individual multimedia instruction model (no collaboration), and The Army School System (TASS), which includes an initial two-week phase conducted in person; a second phase using ADL over approximately eight months; and a third, in-person, phase comparable to the first phase that also lasts two weeks.

CGSS offers AOC using both a traditional resident model taught at Fort Leavenworth and a DL course that was instituted to meet the Army's requirement to educate all majors while accommodating operational staffing requirements. The DL course uses a model that CGSS refers to as blended distributed learning (BDL). Unlike DL that relies heavily on IMI, or most blended-learning (BL) courses, which involve face-to-face interaction, AOC-BDL requires substantial instructor-student and student-student interaction but is completely distributed. That is, the course uses a computer-supported cooperative learning (CSCL) model—comprising a variety of synchronous and asynchronous instructional activities—as well as extensive virtual collaboration among students and instructors who are distributed in space and time. When charged with providing AOC to all Army branch officers in all

---

2 In resident instruction, AOC is the second course in the ILE sequence, which is 44 weeks in total. Resident ILE begins with the Common Core (15.5 weeks), followed by AOC (15.5 weeks), electives (12 weeks), and postprocessing (one week). For students taking the course at a distance, ILE requires only the Common Core and AOC courses.

3 Officers who successfully complete ILE have Military Education Level 4 and Joint Professional Military Education Level 1 designations annotated on their personnel records, which makes them eligible for assignment to many key joint and Army positions.

regions of the world without affecting the personnel operating tempo, CGSS adopted a BDL model as a flexible approach to achieve throughput and meet course goals. However, relatively little is known about the effectiveness of using a fully distributed approach to support the acquisition of critical thinking skills and related competencies.

Prior RAND Arroyo Center research for CGSS has examined the effectiveness of the delivery venues for the ILE Common Core (e.g., Straus and Ward, 2011). The purpose of the current study is to build on this previous work by examining outcomes for AOC-BDL; however, our focus is only on AOC-BDL, not on comparing BDL and resident venues. This project has three central efforts:

- to assess graduates' perceptions of the effectiveness of AOC-BDL, measured both immediately after completing the course and after having an opportunity to apply learned knowledge and skills on the job
- to identify research findings and best practices in CSCL, with a focus on blended DL relevant to AOC-BDL (e.g., adult learners; complex skills)
- to integrate findings from the first two efforts to recommend improvements in course delivery as well as in measurement of student outcomes to assess course effectiveness.

Results of the study will speak to the potential for using BDL in other Army courses with similar learning objectives.

In the remainder of this introduction, we discuss BL in more detail and provide an overview of the framework and approach used in this study.

Understanding Blended Learning

BL is generally considered a way of integrating DL or technologically mediated instructional approaches with in-person activities, such as class discussions, as exemplified in Graham's (2006) definition: "Blended learning systems combine face-to-face instruction with computer-mediated instruction" (p. 4). Typically, BL courses use online activities to replace some, or even most, in-person instruction. Early blended-learning instruction treated face-to-face and technology-mediated learning as separate activities within a course, but current practice tends to integrate the two, to the point where DL instruction makes use of methods that were once possible only in face-to-face classrooms (Graham, 2006).

The move toward online learning has been apparent in higher education more generally, as documented by a recent study of over 2,500 colleges and universities (Allen and Seaman, 2011). Allen and Seaman reported numerous indicators of the prevalence of DL; e.g., they found that chief information officers at 65 percent of reporting institutions consider online learning to be a critical part of their long-term strategy (particularly among public institutions); the rate of growth of online enrollments exceeds the rate of growth of the higher education student population; and 31 percent of all students currently take at least one course online.

Military organizations are also increasingly moving toward DL. Within the Department of Defense (DoD), the ADL Initiative was launched in 1997 to foster the development of guidelines, tools, methodologies, and policies for the cost-effective use of computers in instruction. Over the years, the vision of the ADL initiative has been "to provide access to the highest quality learning and performance aiding that can be tailored to individual needs, and delivered cost-effectively at the right time and at the right place" (Wisher, 2011, p. 3). The results are that DL has increased dramatically within DoD, with service members and DoD civilians completing more than 10 million online courses each year (Wisher, 2011).

Additional evidence documents trends toward BL in particular. Bonk and Graham (2006) documents growth in blended-learning instruction in a variety of universities and corporations. A survey of North American postsecondary institutions (Bonk, Kim, and Zeng, 2006) found that most participants were already using BL in some way in 2003 and anticipated substantial growth in BL instruction in their organizations in the subsequent ten years. Moreover, respondents reported that their preferred pedagogical techniques involve online collaboration, case studies, and problem-based instruction, all of which involve higher levels of learning, such as analysis and synthesis (Bloom, 1956; 1994). On the other hand, learning activities in IMI tend to be limited to lower levels, such as knowledge and comprehension. Although the focus of the present study of AOC is BL at the course level, blending can also occur at the program level; for example, some schools require or allow students to take one or more online courses in addition to their traditional in-person courses (Graham, 2006).

Instructors, programs, or students opt for BL for three primary reasons: improved pedagogy, increased access and flexibility, and improved cost-effectiveness (Graham, Allen, and Ure, 2003, as described in Graham, 2006). BL can improve pedagogy by supporting a wide range of learning methods, including learner-centered strategies and opportunities to connect with representatives from outside organizations, such as guest speakers (Theroux and Kilbane, 2005) and industry partners (e.g., Lockee and Reece, 2005). BL can improve access and flexibility by accommodating students' schedules and providing learning opportunities for students who cannot collocate with instructors and classmates. Unlike IMI, however, BL techniques enable students to have social experiences that emulate in-person classroom activities (Graham, 2006). Finally, BL can be cost-effective for organizations by enabling them to reach a large, distributed student population and through such efficiencies as reduced use of physical facilities and ease of updating course content. Blended approaches can also be cost-effective for students by providing a variety of options for convenient and affordable education.

BDL, which does not include face-to-face activities, is much less common than BL. While BDL has the potential to provide maximum access and flexibility at the lowest cost, it is unclear whether this approach can effectively teach complex material in the absence of face-to-face interaction (see Chapter Four).

Approach Used in This Study

As noted above, this study has three objectives: to assess AOC-BDL effectiveness, to identify best practices in CSCL, and to use findings from these efforts to identify options for improvements in AOC-BDL. We provide an overview of the approaches used to address these objectives below and then describe the conceptual framework used in the study. The methods used in the study are described in more detail in subsequent chapters.

Assessing Advanced Operations Course Effectiveness

To assess AOC-BDL effectiveness, we analyzed responses to exit surveys measuring student satisfaction and perceptions of course quality and impact.[4] We subsequently piloted a survey of AOC-BDL graduates ("postgraduate survey") who completed the 2009–2010 academic year (AY) curriculum sometime in the past two years. The purpose of the postgraduate survey was to collect preliminary data regarding perceptions of course effectiveness among graduates who have had a chance to apply knowledge and skills acquired in AOC on the job, as well as to examine alternatives for question content and format. In addition, CGSS administered an entrance survey to current students that we use to describe the student population and their readiness for AOC-BDL.

Identifying Best Practices in Blended Learning and Computer-Supported Cooperative Learning Applicable to Advanced Operations Course

To identify best practices in CSCL, we reviewed the research literature on BL and conducted original case studies of BL programs.[5] The literature review focused on studies of BL as it is typically implemented (i.e., involving a face-to-face component), distributed BL, and virtual collaboration published from 2007 to 2012. In addition, we reviewed seminal publications on these topics published prior to 2007. We con-

[4] Chapter Three provides additional information on the survey instruments and analysis approach.

[5] Chapter Four provides additional information on the approach we used for the literature review and case studies.

ducted three case studies, one in each of three domains: military education, higher education, and industry training. We supplemented these original case studies with published case studies of BL. Results from these efforts, in combination with our assessment of course effectiveness, were used to address needs for improvement in AOC-BDL course design, delivery, and evaluation.

A Framework for Understanding Online Learning

As a conceptual framework for this study, we adapted Benbunan-Fich, Hiltz, and Harasim's (2005) online interaction learning model to guide our analyses and conclusions. Benbunan-Fich et al. posited that *input factors*, such as technology and course characteristics, influence *learning processes*, which in turn affect *outcomes*, such as learning and satisfaction. We modified the model in several ways to better reflect design and delivery of AOC-BDL and to correspond with concepts found in other input-process-outcome models.[6]

Our working model is shown in Figure 1.1. The figure shows three main types of factors: inputs, learning processes, and outcomes. The items listed under each factor are intended to provide illustrative examples of the types of items within that category; there are others that we have not included, and some of the items included may not pertain to all courses or programs.

The main components of the framework are defined as follows:

- **Inputs:** These comprise all the resources (including people) and contextual factors that contribute to the learning experience, including characteristics of technology, the course, instructors, students, and the organizational context.

[6] Modifications to the Benbunan-Fich et al. model include the following: (a) recategorization of some inputs (for example, the original model classifies the pedagogical approach as an instructor input factor, but CGSS treats the pedagogical approach as a course-level variable); (b) creating a separate input factor for the organization, rather than grouping institutional context with course characteristics; (c) grouping categories within inputs and outcomes, respectively, to depict possible interactions within each construct; and (d) incorporating an arrow allowing for direct effects of inputs on outcomes and a feedback loop indicating that outcomes can influence inputs.

- **Learning processes:** These are the ways through which people learn, e.g., the types and extent of interactions between students and course content, instructors, and other students (e.g., Moore, 1989).
- **Outcomes:** The framework includes the outcomes shown in Figure 1.1 (learning effectiveness, scale or cost-effectiveness, access, student satisfaction, and faculty satisfaction), which reflect the five "pillars" from the Sloan-C quality framework (Sloan Consortium, 2012). In this study, we focused primarily on the two factors shown in italics: learning effectiveness and student satisfaction.[7]

In the figure, we have grouped inputs together to indicate that these variables can affect one another. For example, a student's location can affect bandwidth; connection speed is sometimes slow from locations outside the continental United States (OCONUS). To cite another example, course topics or activities may influence the media mix, that is, topics involving group collaboration may require synchronous technology.

We also posited that some inputs can influence outcomes directly (not only through process), as depicted by the solid arrow; for example, availability and functionality of technology can affect access to courses. The dashed arrow represents a feedback loop to show that outcomes, such as learning effectiveness, can influence inputs, such as student knowledge, skills, and motivation.

In the figure, we have also grouped the outcomes together to indicate that these variables can interact. For example, access might affect learning effectiveness, and learning effectiveness and access might affect student satisfaction.

We describe inputs, learning processes, and outcomes in more detail below.

---

[7] We did not address faculty satisfaction because CGSS evaluates this outcome. Cost-effectiveness and access are important outcomes but were beyond the scope of this study.

Figure 1.1
Framework for Online Learning

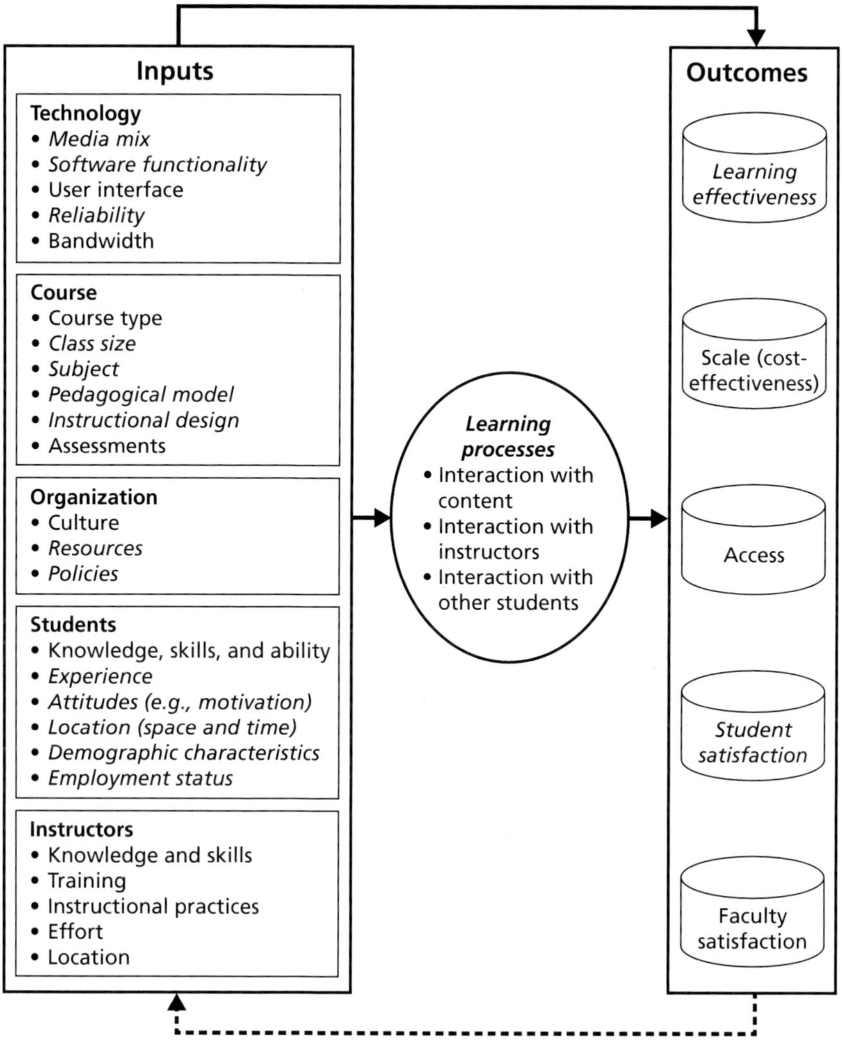

SOURCE: Adapted from Benbunan-Fich, Hiltz, and Harasim, 2005.
RAND *RR172-A-1.1*

Input Factors

Characteristics of *technology* include technical features, such as bandwidth and reliability, and functionality, or what the system allows users to do. The capacity for the technology to bridge time and space (which we consider to be as part of its functionality) determines whether the technology is synchronous or asynchronous. As we describe in more detail in Chapter Two, AOC-BDL uses a combination of synchronous and asynchronous media. Benbunan-Fich, Hiltz, and Harasim (2005) considers the media mix to be the most important aspect of technology for learning.

Course characteristics refer to such factors as subject matter, course type (e.g., required or elective), pedagogical approach, objectives, instructional design, methods of assessment, and class size.[8] In Army training, the pedagogical approach is typically determined at the course level, although instructors in AOC are given latitude to determine some aspects of course delivery.

Student characteristics include such factors as participants' knowledge, skills, abilities, experience, attitudes (including motivation for learning), and demographic characteristics. Such characteristics as knowledge, skills, experience, and attitudes pertain to both the subject matter of the course and media use. We included employment status and student location in this category because they are particularly important in the context of AOC for students in the RC.

Instructor characteristics include knowledge and skills, which likewise pertain to subject matter and use of instructional technology. The extent to which instructors are trained to use these technologies and conduct the course at a distance, as well as their instructional style and the effort they expend while teaching, are other important inputs.

Finally, *organizational characteristics* reflect the institutional context. In the Army, the organization can refer to the college or center or to the Army at large. Examples of relevant organizational characteris-

---

[8] The Quality Matters rubric (Quality Matters Program, 2011) includes a more comprehensive list of course characteristics or standards pertaining to instructional design. These include course overview or introduction, learning objectives, assessment and measurement, instructional materials, learner interaction and engagement, course technology, learner support, and accessibility.

tics include resources, policy (e.g., whether students are provided with dedicated time to participate in training), and culture.

Learning Processes

Benbunan-Fich, Hiltz, and Harasim (2005) identifies a variety of learning processes following Moore (1989), which include student interaction with content, interaction with instructors, and interaction with other students. These processes characterize use of the technology and other learning activities that reflect how students and instructors interact. These processes, which are also referred to as *intervening* or *mediating* variables, can be assessed by measuring communication amount, content, timing, and direction (i.e., who interacts with whom), as well as by socioemotional outcomes, such as trust.

A variety of input factors will influence these types of interactions; for example, the pedagogical model (e.g., collaborative or individual) in combination with student characteristics (e.g., motivation, time zone) and functionalities of technologies (e.g., synchronous or asynchronous) will affect the amount and type of interactions among students (social presence); these factors in combination with instructor characteristics (e.g., degree of knowledge about content and skill in facilitating online interaction) will affect teaching presence; and both sets of factors influence interaction with content.

Outcomes

The outcomes in the model consist of the five "pillars" from the Sloan-C quality framework (Sloan Consortium, 2012). The outcomes, definitions, and examples of measures are shown in Table 1.1.

Our evaluation of AOC-BDL addresses outcomes of learning effectiveness and student satisfaction using analyses of the student surveys. We examined the extent to which outcomes are influenced by features of the technology; student characteristics, such as motivation to take the course; and work and family commitments. Although we do not have direct process measures, student comments and other self-report measures about interaction with instructors and peers speak to the role of these intervening processes.

The case studies and literature review—in combination—address all five input categories and learning processes. With respect to out-

Table 1.1
Five Pillars from the Sloan-C Quality Framework

Outcome	Definition	Measures
Learning effectiveness	Students' mastery of course material meets or exceeds institutional standards	Self-report measures, such as student perceptions of learning and self-efficacy
		Tests of knowledge and skills
		Measures of subsequent job performance
Scale (cost-effectiveness)	Programs and services grow and improve while reducing costs	Program expansion and sustainment
		Return on investment
Access	Students have the opportunity to pursue learning via a wide array of programs and courses	Student self-report
		Indicators of programs and facilities
		Census of services delivered
		Web analytics
Student satisfaction	Students are pleased with their online learning experience	Student and alumni self-report
		Recruitment and retention of students in online courses or programs
Faculty satisfaction	Faculty members are pleased with their experience teaching online	Faculty self-report
		Recruitment and retention of faculty to teach online courses

comes, results from the literature and cases focus primarily on learning effectiveness, access, and student satisfaction, although some findings speak to faculty satisfaction and cost-effectiveness. With some exceptions, the case studies rely on interviewees' descriptions of program or course outcomes, not on quantitative evidence. The literature review fills the gap by supplying results of studies that measure (directly or otherwise) such outcomes as learning effectiveness and student satisfaction. We use the results of the literature review and case studies, in combination with the survey results, to identify how AOC-BDL can alter inputs to improve course processes and outcomes.

Organization of This Report

The remainder of this report is organized as follows:

- In Chapter Two, we set the stage for the analysis by describing AOC-BDL with respect to inputs, such as student population served, instructors, organization, course characteristics, and technologies used.
- In Chapter Three, we describe the survey instruments, analysis approach, and results.
- In Chapter Four, we present the methods and results for the literature review and case studies.
- In Chapter Five, we summarize our findings; present conclusions; and discuss options to improve design, delivery, and evaluation of AOC-BDL.

CHAPTER TWO

The Blended Distributed Learning Advanced Operations Course

AOC focuses on developing the wide range of complex cognitive skills involved in planning military operations collaboratively, with students serving as members of an operational or tactical level staff. Achieving such learning goals is a challenge for any course. Working in an entirely distributed environment poses additional challenges, while offering new opportunities. In this chapter, we focus in particular on the input factors that are central to our analysis, conclusions, and suggested options for improvement in course design and delivery addressed in subsequent chapters of this report. The characteristics include

- **Students:** distributed geographically and across time zones; many have competing demands on their time
- **Instructors:** full-time faculty, mostly Title 10 contract civilians (including retired officers); generalists who teach all topics in the course
- **Organization:** policy requiring AOC completion for promotion; limited opportunities for working on AOC-BDL while on duty status
- **Course:** complex subject matter across multiple echelons; emphasis on collaborative activities; composition of staff groups with diverse skills
- **Technology:** use of synchronous and asynchronous media on DoD networks (dotmil domain).

In this chapter, we describe these and other main inputs that contribute to the AOC-BDL learning experience. This information provides a basis for developing and comparing alternative approaches for improving the delivery of AOC-BDL and its outcomes. We present some information about the AOC course in general and about the Common Core, which is the prerequisite to AOC, but our focus is on the components of the AOC-BDL course.

Sources of information for this effort included: (1) document review, primarily the AOC syllabus, instructional advance sheets, and briefings and papers provided by the CGSS staff,[1] and (2) informal interviews with CGSS staff and faculty members to expand our understanding of what we learned from the document review. We also went through selected IMI or computer-based instruction (CBI) lessons and observed several instructor-student online collaboration sessions.

Students

Most students who take AOC are majors or lieutenant colonels. Resident AOC is taught at Fort Leavenworth, primarily to students in the AC, but AOC-BDL includes students from both the active and reserve components. Data from CGSS indicate that, among 38 recent cohorts, 45 percent of students were in the AC and 56 percent were in the RC. The composition within cohorts varied substantially, however; in approximately one-third of these cohorts, all or most (75 percent or more) students were in the AC; in another one-third, all or most students were in the RC; and in the remaining cohorts, the composition was more mixed.

Because AOC-BDL is entirely distributed, officers take the course where they live or are assigned. Most students complete the course requirements in addition to their normal work or duty day requirements and on weekends. CGSS administered an entrance survey to

---

[1] These included CGSS, 2005; CGSS, 2009; CGSS, 2010, and CGSS 2011. The description of AOC in this chapter outlines the course most students were using during our study period this study. The AOC course has been reorganized somewhat since 2010, but course goals, objectives, and instructional methods remain largely unchanged.

AOC-BDL students in AY 2009–2010 that provides data about their commitments and other demographic characteristics for the cohorts in our evaluation of AOC-BDL.[2] Figure 2.1 shows student age and work and family status.

Although AOC-BDL students have competing demands on their time, they indicated through several items on the entrance survey that they were ready for the course. As shown in Figure 2.2, most students reported having appropriate study habits for a DL course, i.e., being able to work independently, turn in assignments on time, and manage large amounts of reading and writing, and most were ready for the technical aspects of the course in terms of having access to a computer with high-speed Internet and having prior experience with Blackboard, the learning management system (LMS) used in the course. Only about one-half the students, however, had prior experience with Defense Connect Online (DCO), which is the system used for synchronous collaboration (described later in this chapter). Responses to

Figure 2.1
Characteristics of Students in Advanced Operations Course–Blended Distributed Learning

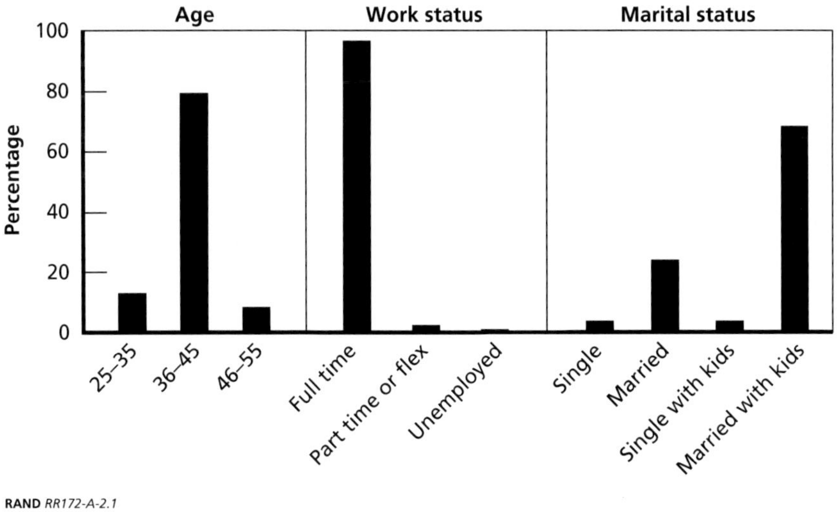

RAND *RR172-A-2.1*

---

[2] Two-hundred and fifteen students completed the entrance survey, for a response rate of 50 percent.

Figure 2.2
Student Readiness for Advanced Operations Course–Blended Distributed Learning

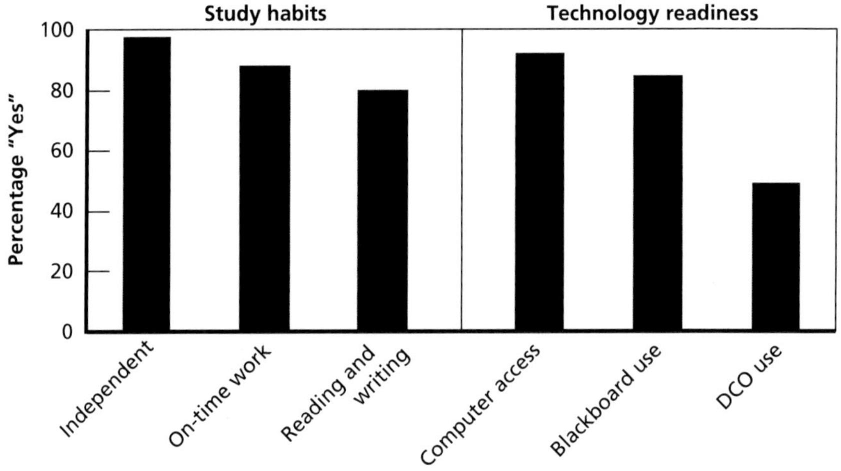

RAND *RR172-A-2.2*

other questions also generally indicate computer readiness; on average, students reported being comfortable using computers and learning new technologies (*M* = 4.05, *SD* = 0.94 on a five-point scale). In addition, students reported that frequent and synchronous interaction with instructions and peers was important (*M* = 3.07, *SD* = 0.62 on a four-point scale), indicating that they had favorable attitudes toward the format of the course.

Instructors

AOC-BDL instructors are full-time faculty, and most are Title 10 contract civilians (most Title 10 instructors are retired officers), with the remainder being officers in the AC. Officers assigned to AOC are Department of the Army–selected, generally for three years. However, CGSS has some authority to review an officer's records before assignment and to select Title 10 instructors for the course.

All instructors receive preparatory training to teach AOC. CGSS has established faculty development programs following Army policy (U.S. Combined Arms Center, 2010). Faculty Development Phase 1 is a two-week course for both resident and BDL course faculty addressing implementation of the experiential learning model. The Phase 2 course provides detailed overviews of delivering particular lessons, typically conducted by the lesson authors. Phase 3 is a workshop focused on lesson design and authoring. In addition, instructors receive substantial training to facilitate online courses, including the Asynchronous Distributed Learning Instructor Course and several days of training on use of Blackboard and DCO. This course lasts four to five weeks and covers a wide range of topics, such as asynchronous learning principles, threaded discussions, learning management systems, course management systems, test design, classroom management, and student performance management.

Unlike their peers in the resident course, who are specialists, AOC-BDL instructors are generalists who teach all topics in the course. To keep faculty up to date, selected instructors are assigned specific course areas and conduct informal faculty development activities on these topics to ensure that the other instructors are knowledgeable and current.

Organization

The Department of Distance Education (DDE) within CGSS executes AOC in the BDL venue. It is also responsible for developing AOC-BDL courseware. In 2010 and 2011, 318 students completed AOC-BDL. In the future, enrollments are expected to be much higher; e.g., the objective for 2013 is 1,160 students. The throughput for AOC-BDL will increase to accommodate a backlog of several thousand students who need to complete the requirement and to ensure that all students can complete AOC prior to promotion.[3]

---

3 Because there is a limit on the number of students in resident AOC (1,440 per year) that will not change, many of the students who need to complete the requirement will take the

Department of the Army policy requires completion of the Common Core and AOC for promotion to lieutenant colonel in the AC and for promotion to colonel in the RC (Department of the Army, 2010). Although AOC is not required for promotion to lieutenant colonel in the RC, completion may increase the RC officer's potential for selection to many career-enhancing assignments, including battalion command. Officers who successfully complete ILE have Military Education Level 4 and Joint Professional Military Education Level 1 designations annotated on their personnel records, and this makes them eligible for assignment to many key joint and Army positions (Department of the Army, 2010).

In contrast to resident AOC (which takes 15.5 weeks to complete), AOC-BDL is designed and scheduled for completion in one year, and extensions of up to six months can be requested and granted on an individual basis. Unlike the resident ILE, which starts twice each year, AOC-BDL student groups are formed and start as students become available. Although AC officers are required to complete both Common Core and AOC in 18 months, RC officers can start AOC several years after completion of the Common Core.[4] Part-time RC students are not formally provided paid duty time to take AOC-BDL, and commanders are not required to allow AC and full-time RC students to take the course on duty time. In contrast, full-time students in the resident course take the course on duty time.[5]

BDL course. In addition, attendance in the resident course will be based on merit.

[4] A long gap between these courses can create a challenge for RC students because some knowledge decay is likely and because AOC builds on learning outcomes in the Common Core. Furthermore, because Army doctrine, equipment, organizations, terms, and planning processes are constantly changing, some material that students learned in the Common Core may be out of date by the time they start AOC.

[5] Similarly, students in the TASS ILE Common Core for the RC can take Phases I and III in a paid active duty for training status and Phase II in a paid inactive duty training status.

Course

Advanced Operations Course Learning Goals

The primary purpose of AOC is to prepare Maneuver, Fires and Effects, and Force Sustainment career field officers and others to serve on battle staffs of operational- and tactical-level headquarters and to develop the professional skills and competencies they will require as field-grade leaders. AOC builds on the Common Core course and develops the officer's abilities to

- analyze complex problems and recommend potential solutions through the application of critical thinking and problem solving models
- build and ethically lead operational and tactical formations in full-spectrum operations in a joint, interagency, intergovernmental, and multinational environment
- analyze the influence of culture and history in military planning and operations
- apply the concepts of joint force deployment and employment at the operational and tactical levels
- communicate effectively
- use historical context to inform military judgment and decision-making.

Blended Distributed Learning Delivery of the Advanced Operations Course

The current AOC-BDL approach was first implemented in 2008. The concept was to use DL to provide a means of instructor and student group collaboration similar to that used in the resident course. Using the resident course as a foundation, instructional designers considered a range of DL methods and used them to design AOC-BDL to reach the same learning goals and objectives. Since its initiation, AOC-BDL has continuously evolved to incorporate lessons learned from ongoing evaluation efforts and to stay up to date with changes to the resident course.

Blocks of Instruction and Learning Objectives

AOC-BDL is organized into six blocks of instruction that have the equivalent of the 308 traditional classroom hours of instruction.[6] The course also requires considerable additional effort, including background reading, individual written assessments, and preparation for classroom-equivalent instruction.[7]

The classroom equivalent hours, the general learning goals, specific learning objectives, and the cognitive level of learning (Bloom, 1956; 1994) associated with each block are described in Appendix A. The three operations blocks, each covering a different operational echelon, represent over 80 percent of the classroom equivalent hours and must be taken sequentially. Although there are individual assignments, students act as members of a group, and most of the students' effort involves collaboratively developing staff products. In contrast, the shorter history and leadership blocks are taken on an individual basis, are conducted in parallel with the operational blocks, and can be taken in any order.

Student Groups

A key element of the instructional approach for the operations blocks is emphasis on collaboration among students and instructors, with a major element being student collaboration to complete group assignments, such as mission analysis briefings and presentation of course-of-action options. To support a collaborative approach, AOC students are organized into 16-person groups called *staff groups*, each of which is composed of officers representing as broad a mix of branches and operational experience as possible. These staff groups stay together for the entire course with the same instructor, and an instructor normally has responsibility for two staff groups. When a student cannot keep up with the group, he or she can apply to be assigned to a subsequent staff group. On average, the course had approximately 25 percent attri-

---

[6] Resident AOC has about the same number of classroom hours but includes a few learning activities (e.g., guest lectures) not included in the BDL venue.

[7] CGSS staff estimates that six hours of work outside of class are required for every four hours in the classroom.

tion over a recent two-year period, so some staff groups were smaller, ranging from eight to 16 students (in contrast to resident instruction, which has very limited attrition). Among students who leave the course, approximately one-half request disenrollment due to military duties, and the remaining students withdraw due to lack of progress.

Achieving diversity in student experience in staff groups is considered to be very important and is prioritized over forming staff groups from proximate geographical locations. Staff groups often contain officers from several time zones, and it is not unusual for one or more of the students to be deployed or stationed in another country. Also, because there are only a few staff groups and a relatively small number of students starting AOC-BDL at any given time, there is less ability to mix student backgrounds in BDL than in the resident course.

For instructional purposes, the 16-person staff group is organized into collaborative teams of different sizes, depending on the specific block and lesson. Sometimes the entire group is organized as a single staff; at other times, it is broken into two eight-person staff groups or four four-person staff groups. The higher the echelon of the headquarters in an activity, the larger the student grouping. For example, for parts of the brigade-focused block, a portion of the student group is organized into four four-person battalion staff groups.

Learning Mechanisms and Supporting Technologies

AOC-BDL uses a combination of synchronous and asynchronous activities, as shown in Table 2.1. The approaches are categorized as either *collaborative* (involving the student interacting with the instructor and/or other students) or *noncollaborative* and either *synchronous* (students and instructor interacting at the same time) or *asynchronous.*

BDL uses different approaches for history and leadership blocks and operations blocks. The history and leadership blocks are asynchronous, and student-instructor interaction is generally limited to the instructor providing written feedback on assignments. In contrast, the operations blocks involve considerable collaboration among students and instructors, including a significant amount that is synchronous. In

Table 2.1
AOC-BDL Approaches

	Asynchronous	Synchronous
Individual	• Readings and study assignments • Written assignments (with instructor feedback) • IMI or CBI • Computer-graded online tests	N/A
Collaborative	• Threaded online discussions • Student-student and student-instructor interaction via email and file-sharing applications	• Student-student and students-instructor sessions and meetings using DCO • Group products and presentations • Conference calls

these blocks, many of the activities are based on Kolb's (1984) Experiential Learning Model, which are learner-centered and "hands-on." The concept is to create an active DL environment in which faculty members are subject-matter experts (SMEs) and facilitators of collaborative learning and in which student-instructor interaction stimulates thought and knowledge construction.

Learning Mechanisms

As shown in Table 2.1, AOC-BDL involves a wide range of individual and collaborative learning mechanisms. We describe these approaches in more detail below, including how these activities contribute to students' grades.

Individual Activities

As in the resident course, students in AOC-BDL are expected to study readings and scenarios out of class. Other individual assignments include online multiple-choice or true/false tests in CBI modules (generally limited to assessing knowledge), written assignments graded by the instructor that include essays, written plans (e.g., a commander's intent statement), and short answer responses.

Collaborative Activities

Although individual activities contribute to students' grades, the majority of students' grades are based on collective activities, with group products in the operational blocks having the greatest weight. AOC-BDL uses a number of different collaborative activities and assignments. Some of these activities, such as DCO sessions and threaded discussions (discussed in more detail later), are used to replace some of the classroom discussions that are part of the resident course.

Operational blocks require approximately 20 synchronous instructor-staff group collaborative sessions. These sessions involve three types of student-instructor interactions: (1) instructor review of course material and discussion of additional points or role plays; (2) presentation of staff group assignments, such as briefings of planning products; and (3) student-instructor discussion of results of student battle plans executed using the Decisive Action simulation (described later in this chapter). These sessions are generally no longer than two hours in length and are scheduled weekly or less frequently. Scheduling is based on student availability (to the extent possible); if a student cannot meet with the group, the instructor will schedule individual makeup sessions or arrange for an alternative activity.

Instructors offer approximately eight optional DCO sessions across the operational blocks. Optional sessions typically are conducted to answer student questions or to allow the instructor to provide additional guidance or discussion of course subject matter.

The group presentations are central to the operations blocks and the course as a whole, comprising 45 to 70 percent of students' course grades. Staff group collaborative efforts to develop team products are the core element of the AOC-BDL approach. A different staff group leader is assigned for each effort, and the instructor coordinates with the leader to ensure that each member of the group has specific responsibilities. During the DCO session, each student presents and defends his or her portion of the group effort. For most group efforts, each student normally receives an individual grade, but in some cases, members of a group may receive the same grade.

Threaded online discussions are used to supplement CBI instruction and are the primary determinant of class participation grades (in addition, an extended operations exercise conducted via DCO contributes to participation grades). Typically the instructor presents a question to the group in an online forum on the LMS and all students are required to respond. The instructor monitors responses and asks students to comment on others' responses.

Informal asynchronous student-student and student-instructor interaction is common, especially in the development of group products. These interactions typically occur via DCO, email, or phone. If a group desires, instructors can participate, and if conducted on DCO, the instructor can review recorded sessions.

Technology

A range of technologies supports synchronous and asynchronous instruction, including Blackboard's LMS, DCO, IMI/CBI, "serious games," and other communication media. Technologies that are supported by CGSS, including Blackboard LMS, DCO, and milSuite, run in a dotmil domain. Some of these course technologies were referred to in the previous section; here, we describe the media in more detail.[8]

Blackboard Learning Management System

Most of the DL components used in the course are supported by Blackboard's LMS, which has been configured to meet specific ILE requirements.[9] Through this system, students can take CBI lessons; review reading materials, scenarios, and other background materials; take online tests; submit and receive written assignments; participate in threaded discussions; exchange papers and products; and track their progress. Likewise, the system allows instructors to track student progress.

DCO is a DoD online collaboration site that supports synchronous collaboration. It includes the DCO Portal, a version of Adobe's

---

8 A small number of staff groups have adopted milSuite, which is a set of social media applications that support such collaborative activities as blogging, discussion boards, a shared calendar for planning events, and a tool for tracking progress on group projects; milSuite also has an online wiki, but CGSS currently is not licensed to use it for AOC.

9 Blackboard Inc. is an enterprise software company that develops educational software, in particular, learning management systems.

Acrobat Connect web conferencing tool, and Jabber instant messaging. DCO provides screen-sharing, whiteboarding, integrated Voice over Internet Protocols, and instant messaging capabilities to support collaboration. DCO sessions can be recorded and reviewed later.

Interactive Multimedia Instruction or Computer-Based Instruction

AOC's IMI or CBI consists mainly of narrated text and chart screen shots and a few videos. These sessions focus on the knowledge elements needed for completion of the higher cognitive block requirements. CBI instruction includes automated and ungraded checks on learning, including multiple-choice questions and activities, such as "drag and drop" exercises in which students match an answer from a group of responses to a group of categories and then receive feedback on that answer (whether right or wrong). There are almost 50 CBI sessions, each about one hour long, covering almost all lessons in the course.

Decisive Action is a simulation that allows the DDE staff to run students' plans in a division and corps level combat exercise. The students can then see their plans worked against a simulated opponent.

Students also use other media to collaborate in ways that are practical for the group members. As we will describe in more detail in Chapter Three, students frequently communicate via email and telephone and make use of file-sharing applications in addition to Blackboard (e.g., Google Docs and SharePoint). Few students report using other technologies (e.g., Skype, face-to-face interaction, social media).

Conclusion

In this chapter, we have described the key input factors in AOC-BDL. These factors have established the foundation for the discussion presented in the next chapter, which discusses outcomes regarding student satisfaction and learning effectiveness in AOC-BDL and the ways in which inputs and learning processes influence these outcomes in the course.

CHAPTER THREE

Satisfaction and Perceived Learning Effectiveness in the Blended Distributed Learning Advanced Operations Course

In this chapter, we describe findings from an exit survey administered to students at the end of AOC-BDL, as well as results from a pilot test of a survey given to graduates of AOC-BDL sometime after completing the course (the postgraduate survey).

We present findings regarding course outcomes in terms of both student satisfaction and perceived learning effectiveness. Subsequently, we diagnose needs for improvement in the course by examining results regarding collaboration (learning processes) and technology and student characteristics (inputs). We conclude with findings that integrate measures of inputs, processes, and outcomes. Components of the framework highlighted in this chapter are shown in italics in Figure 3.1.

Student surveys are the most common method of evaluating training and education. Surveys can be used to measure many aspects of education, such as perceived learning effectiveness; perceptions about the learning process; access; and satisfaction with course design and delivery, instructor style, organizational support, and other factors. Surveys also can be used to collect data about input variables, such as student characteristics. Although student perceptions are not objective measures of learning or course quality, they provide valuable information that can be used to identify needs for improvement (e.g., Sitzmann et al., 2008). Moreover, student reactions can be correlated with other evaluation outcomes, including objective measures of learning, such as

Figure 3.1
Elements of Learning Model Addressed in Analyses of Student Surveys

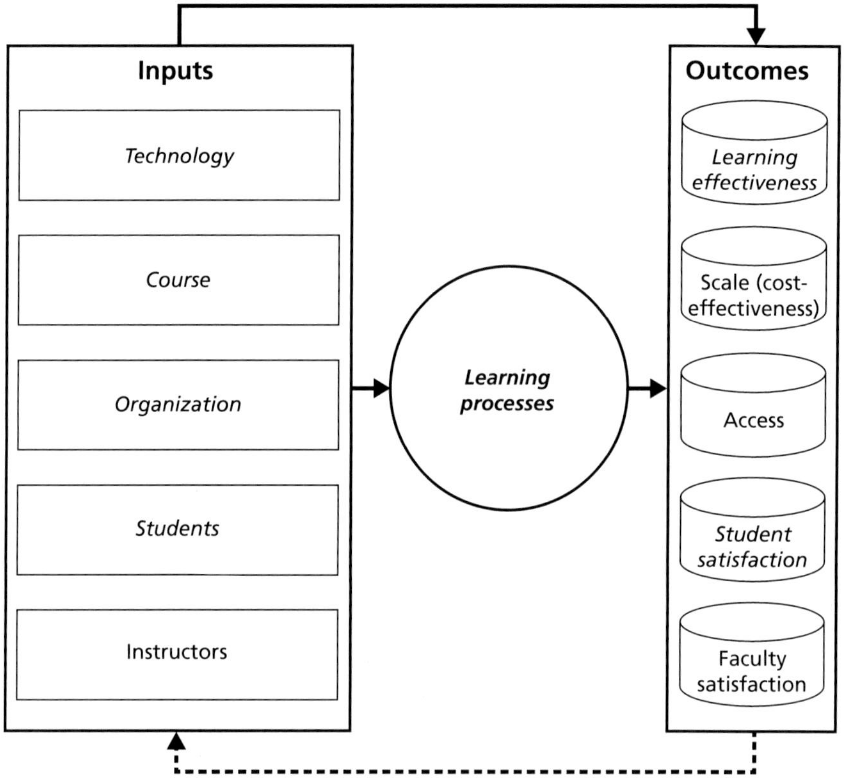

RAND *RR172-A-3.1*

learning and transfer performance (Alliger et al., 1997) and posttraining declarative and procedural knowledge (Sitzmann et al., 2008).

Table 3.1 summarizes the key findings from our analyses.

Methods and Approach

Students complete an exit survey at the end of AOC-BDL that measures their perceptions of learning effectiveness and satisfaction with a variety of aspects of the course, as well as select demographic characteristics. The exit survey is particularly important in the present analy-

Table 3.1
Major Findings from Surveys

Model Component	Major Findings
Outcomes	Students were generally satisfied with the course and learning environment. However, 50 percent of students in the exit survey and 29 percent of postgraduates said they would not recommend the course to others.
	Students felt the course prepared them to lead in Army and joint environments, less so in international and interagency domains.
	Students felt the course was more effective for acquiring substantive knowledge than for development of critical field-grade skills. Only 40 to 50 percent of graduates reported moderate or substantial improvement in these skills.
	Students' ratings of AOC-BDL appear to have been influenced by the student's original Common Core venue, with the highest ratings of AOC-BDL from students who took the Common Core via ADL and the lowest ratings from students who took the Common Core via resident instruction.
Learning Processes	Students identified problems with computer-supported collaboration for learning.
	Students noted that the completely distributed environment did not support some course goals. Specific technologies, especially DCO, interfered with learning processes.
	Students had more favorable responses regarding instructor-student interaction than student-student interaction. Free riding and difficulties scheduling time for synchronous collaboration in student groups were central issues.
Inputs	The reliability of technology posed problems for some students.
	Student motivation for taking AOC-BDL and other commitments (work/family) may constrain participation or engagement in the course.

sis because it serves as the primary means of course evaluation. We supplemented these data with responses to a pilot survey of AOC-BDL (the postgraduate survey) administered to officers who had completed AOC-BDL and returned to their units. This survey was designed to test some of RAND Arroyo Center's proposed suggestions to improve the exit survey and to begin to understand the effectiveness of AOC for students who have had a chance to apply the knowledge and skills they gained from the course to their jobs.

We were not able in this effort, however, to survey the 25 percent of students who dropped out of the course before its conclusion. In general, we would expect these students to report lower learning effectiveness and satisfaction ratings than students who did finish. One of our recommendations (described in Chapter Five) is for CGSS to collect feedback about the course from students who drop out.

Both the exit and postgraduate surveys were administered to students who completed the AY 2009–2010 curriculum. All surveys were administered via the school's Blackboard LMS. Students completed the surveys anonymously.

Exit Survey

The exit survey consisted of 63 items, including 60 closed-ended questions and three open-ended questions. Closed-ended questions measured the following topics:

- satisfaction with the virtual classroom environment, as well as general satisfaction
- learning effectiveness in terms of achievement of substantive content (e.g., "Completing AOC prepared me to apply Battle Command systems") and attainment of critical field-grade competencies, such as improved critical thinking and communication skills
- technology availability and reliability
- demographic and background characteristics.

Most closed-ended questions measuring satisfaction and learning effectiveness used five-point Likert-type scales ranging from "strongly disagree" to "strongly agree," with the midpoint of the scale defined as "neither agree nor disagree." Items measuring access used yes-or-no responses, and additional questions used other formats, such as rankings or other multiple choices.

Open-ended questions solicited comments and recommendations regarding course content; recommendations to improve other aspects of the course; and, for students who reported that the course did not meet its core objective, reasons for their response. One hundred and thirty-seven out of 165 students (83 percent) answered at least one open-ended question; 93 students (56 percent) answered two or three questions. Many students wrote lengthy responses and offered numerous comments and recommendations. Responses were coded by topic and by the sentiment (positive or negative), as described later in this chapter.

Postgraduate Survey

The postgraduate survey was designed to collect data regarding issues raised in students' open-ended responses that were not measured elsewhere in the exit survey and that correspond to key goals or design elements of the course. In particular, the survey included closed-ended questions measuring collaborative learning processes, as well as student characteristics to better explain ratings of satisfaction and learning effectiveness. The survey was also used to examine alternative numbers and labels of response options and to obtain preliminary data about the value of AOC-BDL from officers after returning to their units. The survey consisted of 36 closed-ended questions and three open-ended questions. Closed-ended questions addressed the following topics:

- student characteristics
- learning effectiveness with respect to critical field grade competencies and CBI
- media used to collaborate and perceptions of collaboration and group processes
- technology reliability
- general satisfaction.

Most of the questions on the postgraduate survey were new or substantially revised from the exit survey. The survey was also designed to be narrowly focused in keeping with the goals described above. With the exception of general satisfaction questions, most results are not comparable between the exit and postgraduate survey because of differences in question content, response options, or both.

Response options for questions about learning effectiveness and satisfaction consisted of six-point Likert-type scales ranging from "strongly disagree" to "strongly agree" (with no midpoint) or four-point scales regarding learning effectiveness (i.e., from "not at all" to "substantial"). We used six-point scales with no midpoint in an attempt to reduce leniency bias observed in surveys of students in the Common Core (Straus and Ward, 2011). Results presented in Appendix B suggest less leniency bias with the six-point scales. Other questions used different multiple choice options (e.g., for barriers: not at all, somewhat, a great extent).

Open-ended questions solicited comments about the effectiveness of collaboration methods; recommendations to improve collaboration; and, for students who reported that they would not recommend the course to others, the reasons for their response. We discuss some responses to these questions, but they were not coded systematically in our analysis.

Presentation of Survey Results

The results presented in this chapter are based on responses from both the exit and postgraduate surveys. In some cases, we intersperse findings from both surveys to address particular inputs or outcomes or to present comparative findings. Table 3.2 summarizes key features of these two surveys. Bar charts depicting results are presented in solid gray scale for the exit survey and in crosshatch patterns for the postgraduate survey.

Table 3.2
Summary of Exit and Postgraduate Surveys

	Survey	
Factor	**Exit**	**Postgraduate**
When administered	End of course	1 to 23 months postgraduation
How surveys differ from each other	• More questions • Mostly five-point agree/disagree scales	• Fewer questions • More pointed questions and response options • Mostly four- and six-point scales
Number of responses (response rate)	165 (74 percent)	126 (34 percent)
Answered at least one open-ended question	83 percent	90 percent

Survey Respondents

At the time we received exit survey data, 223 students had completed the course. One-hundred and sixty-five students completed the survey, for a 74 percent response rate. The sample size in each analysis varied somewhat due to missing responses. Three hundred and sixty-seven graduates who completed the AY 2009–2010 AOC-BDL curriculum were recruited via email to participate. One hundred and twenty-six graduates completed the survey, for a response rate of 34 percent.[1]

Because participation was anonymous, we could not link responses across surveys. Therefore, although responses to the entrance survey could be used to characterize students in the course, they could not be used to help us better understand student evaluations of the course (e.g., whether satisfaction with the course or perceived learning varied based on prior DL experience, age, marital status, etc.). Student characteristics could be used as "moderator" or explanatory variables of satisfaction or other outcomes only if both sets of variables were measured in the same survey (which was primarily for the postgraduate survey).

Survey Measurement Characteristics

Appendix B presents psychometric properties of the items and information about response sets (i.e., patterns of responding that may not be indicative of respondents' true attitudes). For the exit survey, internal consistency reliability, as measured by coefficient alpha, ranged from 0.82 to 0.97. For the postgraduate survey, coefficient alpha ranged from 0.75 to 0.93. As described in Appendix B, there may have been some leniency bias in the exit survey but somewhat less leniency bias in postgraduate responses. Answers in the exit survey (which was lengthy) did not seem to show response fatigue or careless responding in that there was variability in students' answers.

---

[1] Response rates likely differ because the exit survey is considered a requirement, and completion of the survey is documented in the LMS grade book (documentation occurs automatically because the survey is implemented within the same LMS). In contrast, the postgraduate survey was entirely voluntary, and there was no documentation of who did or did not participate.

Outcomes

In this section, we present findings from the surveys, beginning with student satisfaction and perceived learning effectiveness (outcomes). Next, we discuss collaboration (learning processes), followed by analyses of technology and student characteristics (inputs). We conclude with analyses of relationships among these factors.

Students Were Generally Satisfied with the Course and Learning Environment

Figure 3.2 shows responses to a question in the exit survey regarding whether students felt that AOC achieved its core purpose. Close to 80 percent of the students responded "yes," indicating that, overall, most students felt that the course was successful. However, the rates of "somewhat" responses indicate some need for improvement.

Figure 3.3 shows responses to questions about student satisfaction with the virtual learning environment and general satisfaction with the course. Although responses can be analyzed based on average ratings, we present percentages of "agree" (agree or strongly agree), "neutral" (neither agree nor disagree), and "disagree" (disagree or strongly disagree) responses to depict the degree of variability in students' views

Figure 3.2
Achievement of Core Purpose—Exit Survey

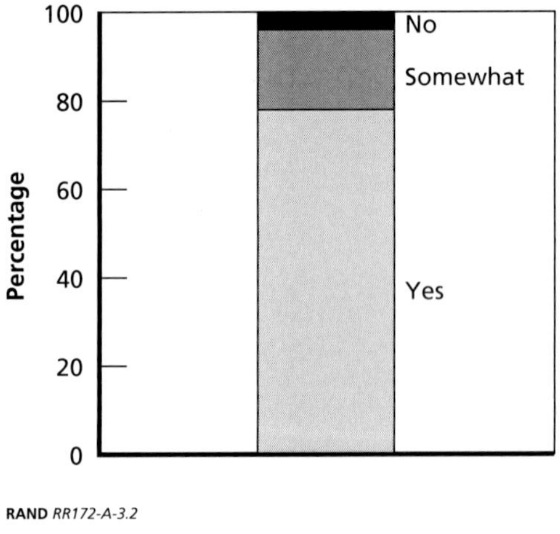

Figure 3.3
Satisfaction with Virtual Learning Environment and General Satisfaction with the Course—Exit Survey

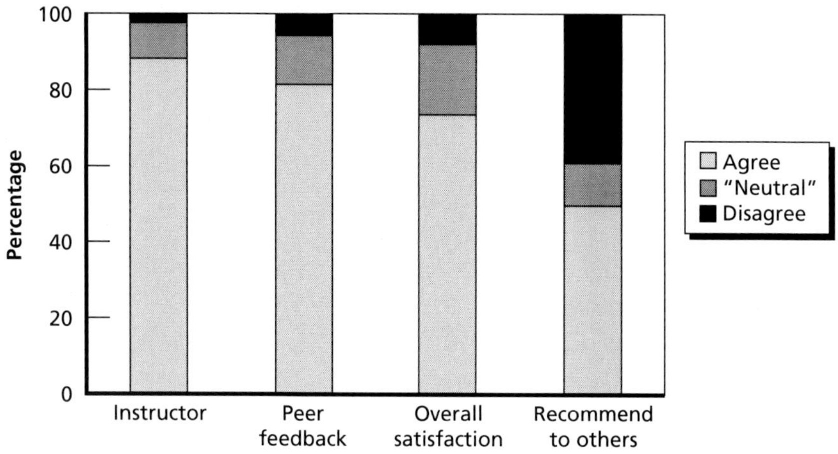

RAND *RR172-A-3.3*

(mean responses can be in found in Appendix B). Responses show that most students were satisfied with aspects of the learning environment, such as quality of instruction and peer interaction and feedback, and that they were generally satisfied with the course overall.

Responses to open-ended questions illustrate students' perceptions of instructors. For example:

> Mr. [ ] was very prompt with his critiques and provided direct, but much needed constructive criticism to the assigned work. He is a highly professional and very effective instructor.

> Dr. [ ] did a great job of working with the class no matter the schedule to make it functional. I recommend that all the instructors understand that life happens, and flexibility is a must. AOC is important to the students or we would not have invested the time to enroll. Glad I took the class, learned a ton, have great products that I can use in the future. Thanks.

Other comments illustrate that students valued the feedback they received through peer collaboration:

> The greatest benefit from the course was collaboration with the members of the cohort with diverse backgrounds and experiences. Collaborative assignments were the most difficult, but the most beneficial.
>
> Highly encourage future students to do as much collaboration work, work projects, etc. with other members of the group in the DCO sessions.
>
> More DCO sessions; interaction among the students was crucial to professional development in the course.

Despite Overall Satisfaction, 50 Percent of Students Said They Would Not Recommend the Course to Others

Despite satisfaction with the learning environment and with the course in general, only 50 percent of students reported that they would recommend the course to others. Likewise, even among students who felt that AOC achieved its core purpose, over 30 percent reported that they would not recommend the course to others (see Figure 3.4). Possible reasons for these responses are explored later in this chapter.

Figure 3.4
Ratings of Recommending Course to Others Based on Views That the Advanced Operations Course Achieved Its Core Purpose—Exit Survey

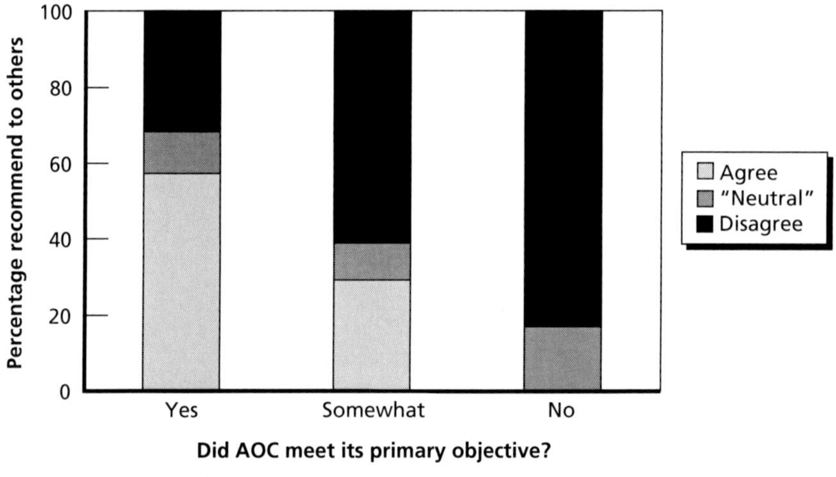

RAND *RR172-A-3.4*

We compared ratings of satisfaction and recommending the course to others from the exit and postgraduate surveys.[2] Figure 3.5 shows the distributions of responses to these questions. Because the exit and postgraduate surveys used different response scales (five- and six-point response options, respectively), responses were converted to a common scale ranging from –2 to +2 following Adelson and McCoach (2010) (see Figure 3.6).[3] Repeated-measures analyses of variance show that there were no differences between the average ratings of satisfaction for students surveyed at the end of the course and those surveyed

Figure 3.5
Satisfaction and Recommending Advanced Operations Course to Others—Exit and Postgraduate Surveys

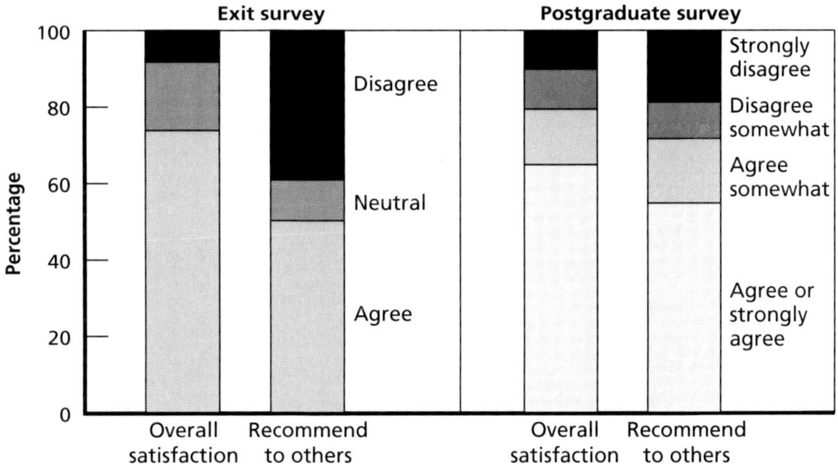

RAND *RR172-A-3.5*

---

2 In the postgraduate survey, responses to the question about recommending the course to others were correlated with other satisfaction items; however, this item is presented separately here to compare results with exit survey responses.

3 Responses to these items were converted so that they spanned the same range to make comparisons of means and standard deviations meaningful. For the exit survey, responses were coded such that –2 = strongly disagree, –1 = disagree, 0 = neither agree nor disagree, 1 = agree, and 2 = strongly agree. For the postgraduate survey, –2 = strongly disagree, –1.2 = disagree, –0.4 = disagree somewhat, 0.4 = agree somewhat, 1.2 = agree, and 2 = strongly agree.

Figure 3.6
Satisfaction and Recommending the Course to Others—Rescaled Ratings from Exit and Postgraduate Surveys

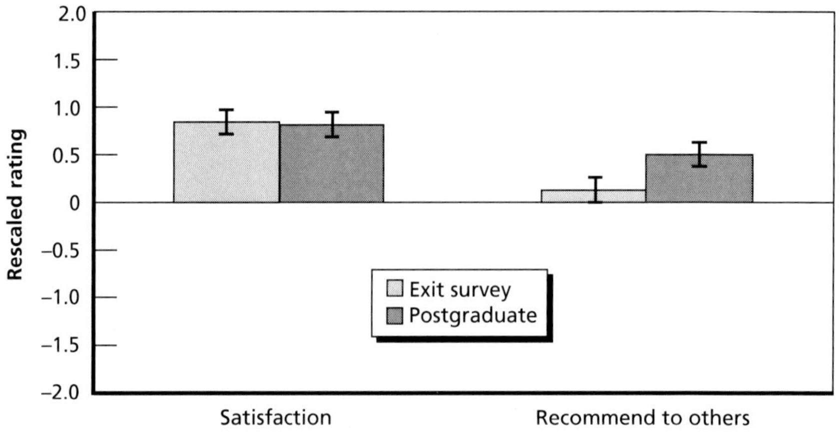

NOTE: $p < 0.05$.
RAND *RR172-A-3.6*

postgraduation, although postgraduates had more-favorable reactions regarding recommending AOC-BDL to others.[4]

Students Felt the Course Prepared Them to Lead in Army and Joint Environments, Less So in International and Interagency Domains

We now describe results regarding perceived learning effectiveness. An item on the exit survey asked students if AOC prepared them to operate as a commander or staff officer in several different environments. Figure 3.7 shows the percentages of students who reported "yes" and "no" for each environment. Most students reported that the course prepared them to lead in Army and joint environments, but students felt less prepared for operations in multinational and interagency domains.

---

4 For overall satisfaction, $F(1,286) < 1$; for recommending the course to others, $F(1,286) = 5.23$, $p < 0.05$. There was a main effect for survey group (i.e., with higher ratings from respondents in the postgraduate survey), $F(1,286) = 85.45$, $p < 0.001$, and an interaction of survey group and item, such that the discrepancy between satisfaction and recommending the course to others was much smaller for postgraduate survey respondents than for exit respondents, $F(1,286) = 12.63$, $p < .001$.

Figure 3.7
Preparation to Lead in Different Environments—Exit Survey

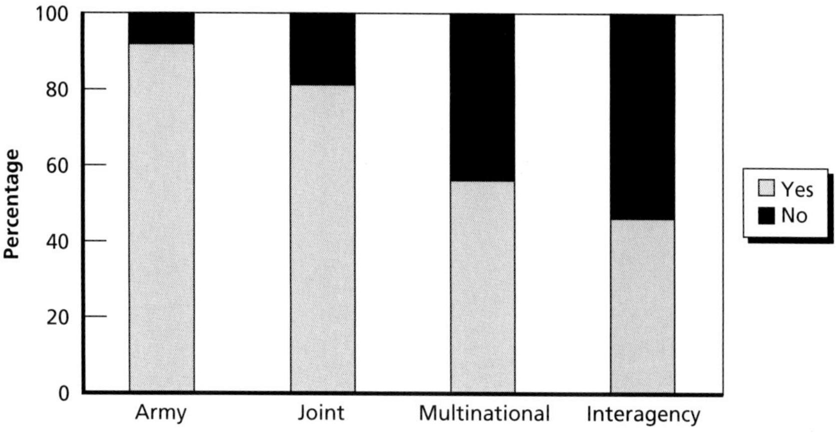

RAND *RR172-A-3.7*

Students Felt the Course Was More Effective for Acquisition of Substantive Knowledge than for Development of General Critical Field-Grade Skills

Figure 3.8 shows exit survey ratings of the extent to which students perceived the course to be successful in fostering learning of topics taught primarily via CBI (history and leadership); operational topics, such as understanding joint force capabilities and limitations, the joint operational planning process, and change management processes; and general critical field-grade competencies, such as critical thinking and communication skills. Results show that students gave generally favorable ratings to history and to operations topics. Ratings were somewhat lower for leadership and critical thinking skills and substantially lower for the degree to which students felt that the course improved their written and oral communication skills. Analysis of variance of the association of beliefs about whether the course met its core purpose with these ratings of learning effectiveness shows that students who reported that the course did not meet its core purpose had much lower ratings of learning effectiveness across all topics, as indicated by the asterisks in Figure 3.9. In contrast, there were no differences in perceptions of the learning environment based on whether students felt the

Figure 3.8
Achievement of Academic Objectives—Exit Survey

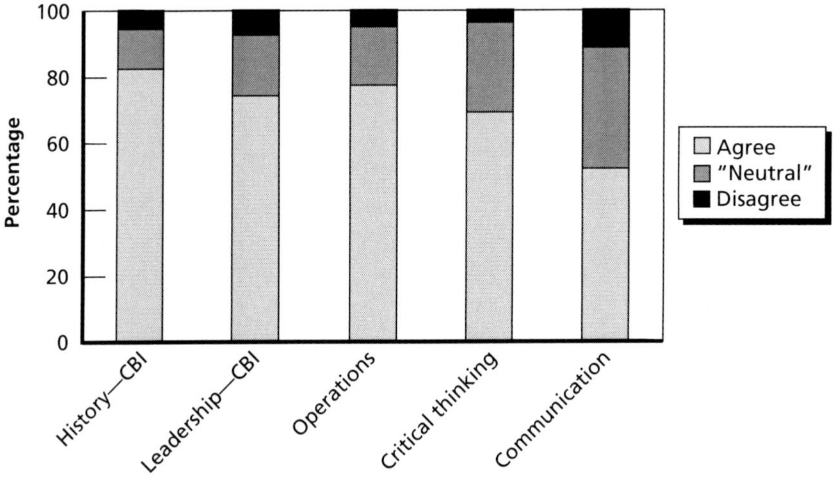

RAND *RR172-A-3.8*

course achieved its core purpose. This suggests that learning effectiveness may "drive" views of overall success of the course, although we note that these data are correlational rather than causal.

Forty to 50 Percent of Graduates Reported Moderate or Substantial Improvement in Critical Field-Grade Skills

In the postgraduate survey, questions about learning effectiveness addressed learning from CBI (history and leadership) and acquisition of general critical field-grade competencies (but not operations). Fifty-two percent of graduates agreed or strongly agreed that the CBI lessons contributed to achieving course learning objectives, and an additional 29 percent agreed somewhat. In contrast to the exit survey, in which students were asked whether the course helped improved their critical field-grade skills (using agree or disagree scales), achievement of these skills in the postgraduate survey was assessed with items asking about the degree to which the course improved their abilities with respect to using the military decision making process (MDMP), complex problem solving, organizational leadership, and oral and written communication. Response options ranged from "not at all" to "a substantial

Figure 3.9
Average Ratings of Learning Environment and Achievement of Academic Objectives Based on Perceptions That the Advanced Operations Course Achieved Its Core Purpose—Exit Survey

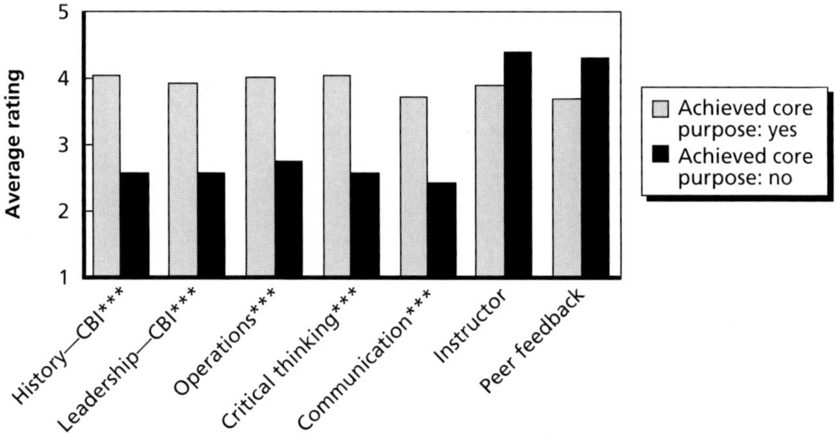

NOTE: *** indicates that all differences were statistically significant at $p < .001$. For ratings of academic objectives, all differences between groups responding "yes" and "no" were statistically significant. With the exception of "history," there were also significant differences in ratings between "yes" and "somewhat" groups. Differences between "somewhat" and "no" groups were not significant for leadership or communication.

RAND *RR172-A-3.9*

amount." Although these four items formed a coherent scale (coefficient alpha = 0.89), we report results for individual items below (see Figure 3.10). Results show that only 40 to 50 percent of graduates reported moderate to substantial improvement in these competencies. The mean rating was 2.45 (*SD* = 0.75) on a four-point scale.

Student Ratings of the Advanced Operations Course Appear to Be Influenced by Their Original Common Core Venue

Another question in the postgraduate survey asked respondents to compare the instructional methods in AOC-BDL with what they had experienced in the Common Core. Response options ranged from one ("much worse") to five ("much better"), with a midpoint corresponding to "about the same." Overall, 66 percent of graduates reported that the delivery method for AOC-BDL was better or about the same as the

Figure 3.10
Postgraduate Achievement of Critical Field-Grade Competencies

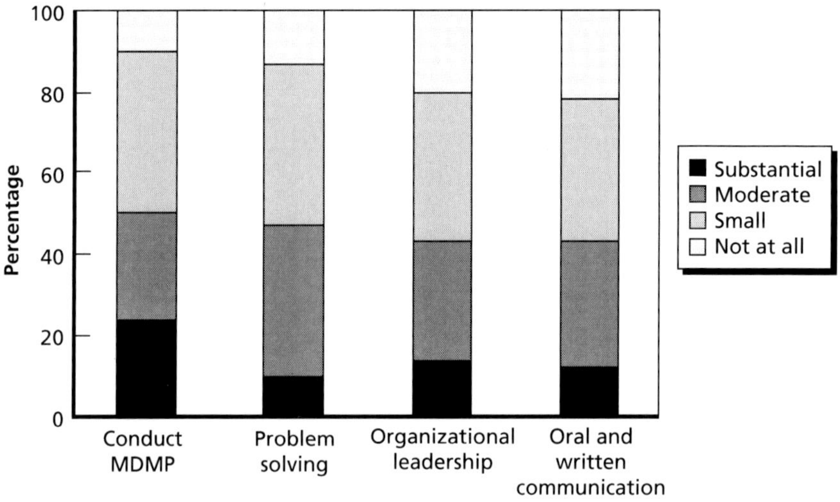

RAND *RR172-A-3.10*

Common Core. However, this result differed by Common Core venue. Figure 3.11 shows responses based on the venue in which graduates had taken the Common Core—ADL, TASS, or resident instruction in satellite locations.[5] For this analysis, responses were reduced to three categories, i.e., better, about the same, or worse. Results show a significant interaction between original Common Core venue and comparative ratings of AOC-BDL, with more favorable ratings of AOC-BDL among graduates who had taken the Common Core via ADL and the least favorable ratings among graduates who had taken the Common Core in residence, ($\chi^2_{(4)} = 10.02, p < 0.05$).

These findings point to two conclusions. First, while a majority of students believe AOC-BDL is better than, or about the same as, the Common Core, there is a substantial difference of opinion among students who took the resident course, with close to one-half believing that the instructional delivery in resident instruction was superior

[5] This analysis omits respondents who said that they switched between ADL and TASS during the Common Core.

Figure 3.11
Postgraduates' Retrospective Comparisons of Advanced Operations Course Blended Distributed Learning with Common Core Based on Common Core Venue

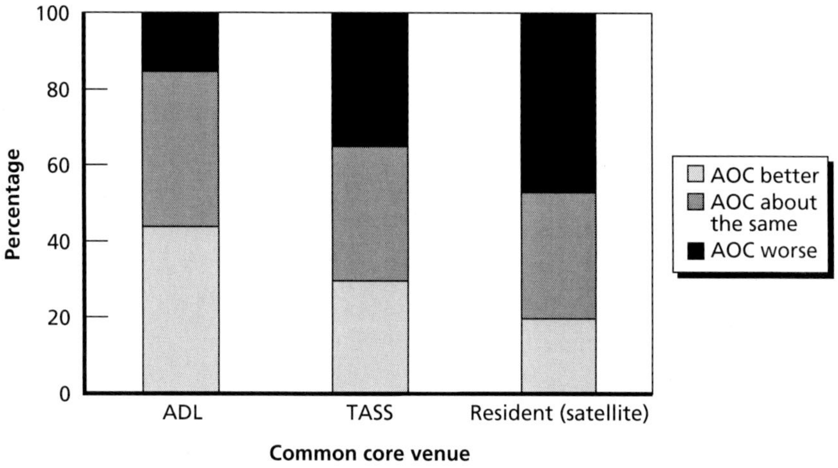

RAND *RR172-A-3.11*

to that in AOC-BDL. Second, the comparison among students who took the ADL Common Core course could be interpreted as a need for change in the ADL Common Core, i.e., to move from strict IMI to a blended format. These conclusions are addressed in more detail in Chapter Five.

Learning Processes

Students' Comments Note Problems with Computer-Supported Collaboration for Learning

We looked at collaborative processes as a possible explanation for the outcomes described above. The exit survey included an item that asked students whether online tools, such as discussion boards, wikis, DCO, and blogs, enhanced their learning. Sixty-three percent of students reported "agree" responses; 13 percent disagreed; and 24 percent were neutral. Although most students appeared satisfied with these technologies, there was only a single question about the value of online tools, despite their central role in supporting collaboration in AOC-BDL. Moreover, responses to open-ended questions illuminate a number of issues with computer-supported collaboration in the course.

As described earlier, responses to open-ended questions in the exit survey were coded with respect to topic and sentiment.[6] The most frequently mentioned topics are defined in Table 3.3. Figure 3.12 shows the frequencies of positive and negative comments for these topics. The total number, rather than percentage, of comments is shown because students often commented on multiple topics. The overwhelming finding from this analysis is the sheer number of comments about learn-

Table 3.3
Frequently Mentioned Topics in Open-Ended Responses

Topic	Definition
Computer-supported cooperative learning (CSCL) approach	Comments about the CSCL approach used in the course, including remarks about collaboration and/or technology for collaboration
Time requirements	Amount of time required to work on the course
General comments (General)	General statements, such as "This was a good course"
Instructor	Comments about the instructor, e.g., quality of instructional delivery or knowledge, availability, quality of feedback
Course structure or length	Structure of the course, such as order of topics or course length
Expectations	Extent to which students had realistic expectations about course requirements
Assignments	Remarks about written assignments, presentations, etc.
Senior mentors	Suggestions to provide senior mentors to students
Master's degree	Comments about providing master's degree credit for course completion
Other	Miscellaneous comments that occurred infrequently

[6] Sixty-two students recommended changes in course content or assignments, but we did not code the specific topics addressed in their comments for this evaluation.

Figure 3.12
Frequencies of Positive and Negative Comments—Exit Survey

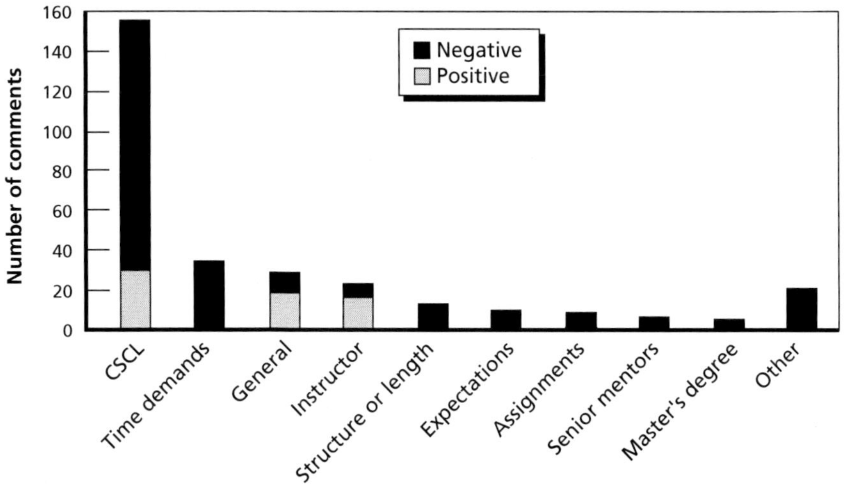

RAND *RR172-A-3.12*

ing processes, particularly collaboration, and views regarding the influence of these processes on learning effectiveness. Although there were a number of positive comments, mostly emphasizing the value of collaboration and/or calling for more DCO sessions, we surmise that the prevalence of the negative reactions to a CSCL approach may explain why a large percentage of students reported that they would not recommend the course to others.

A number of students had positive general comments to the course, stating that it was effective overall and that the content was useful. Responses were often qualified, however, with concerns about course design or delivery and recommendations for improvement. The following quotations are typical of many of the comments that students provided. Students often addressed multiple issues, including the quality of collaboration, technology reliability and access, competing demands on their time (i.e., "local priorities"), complexity of the coursework, and the challenges of working across time zones. A number of students emphasized the need for face-to-face interaction;

the most common recommendation was to have a one- to two-week in-person exercise at the end of the course.

> Schedule TDY [temporary duty] for large assignments where coordination between peers is essential to learning. O200 and O300 courses needed better interaction on a daily basis, not sporadic interaction over a flawed DCO connection. . . . I thought we could have learned a lot more from each other than some of the assignments allowed over distance learning.

> Incorporate a one to two week resident culmination exercise. . . . coordinating with ten or more people remotely to produce a decent division OPORD [operational order] is somewhat low in utility without the face-to-face interaction. The effort is diluted by the need to constantly factor in numerous different time zones, local priorities, and access to the network.

The second most frequently mentioned topic was the amount of time required for the course. Comments indicated that students had substantial commitments that interfered with their ability to spend adequate time on the course, and these officers were not given dedicated time to work on AOC. The result was that students felt they could not devote sufficient attention to the course and/or to their jobs or other commitments. For example,

> [F]inding equal time during and after hours to complete the AOC portion coupled with a deployment for the final 3 & 1/2 months was just very taxing. I would, and have, recommended to others to attend the resident course and be a fulltime student for 11 months vice [sic] my experience.

> This class required way too much outside time and effort on my behalf. This was difficult as a Reservist trying to not only hold down a civilian job, unit/reserve obligations and other outside family obligations.

> Being deployed puts a major strain on a student's ability to participate in DCO sessions and distracts you from the true mission at hand.

> AOC became a distraction from my job rather than a learning experience. I had a staff job that demanded a great deal of my time; to compensate, I did the minimum for AOC—I passed the quizzes and did my assignments. The only assignments I ensured got my full attention were the group assignments because other people were counting on me; otherwise I did what I had to do to get a "Go." That is not the attitude I had during the Common Core while at the satellite resident phase. During Common Core, I gave it my best shot because that was my place of duty and there were no conflicting missions.

Student's Comments Emphasized That a Completely Distributed Environment Posed Challenges for Meeting Some Course Goals

Given the number of comments about the CSCL approach, we broke down students' comments about collaborative learning processes into subcategories to better understand their concerns. Figure 3.13 shows the negative sentiments about these topics. The first four bars in the

Figure 3.13
Specific Categories of Negative Comments About Computer-Supported Cooperative Learning—Exit Survey

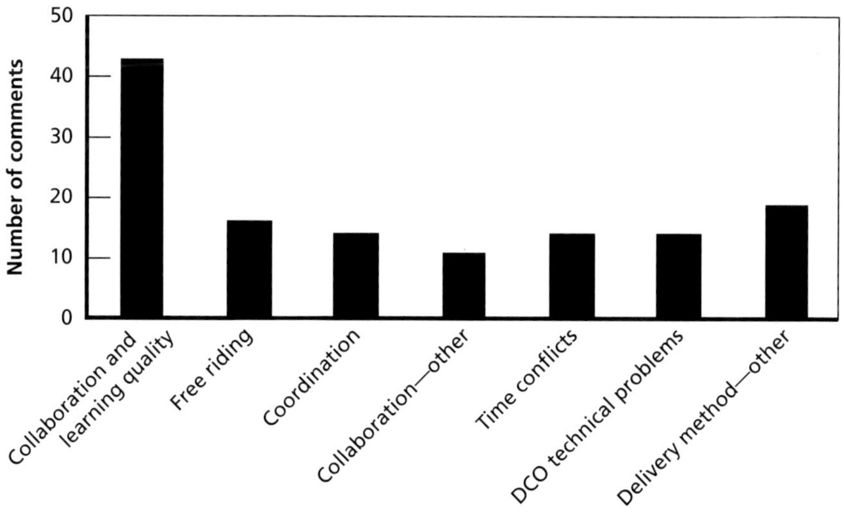

RAND *RR172-A-3.13*

figure pertain to collaboration, followed by issues of conflicting commitments, technology reliability, and other issues.

Here, the most common topic was the extent to which the BDL approach supported collaboration and learning. The preponderance of comments emphasized that the completely distributed environment impeded some course learning goals, such as MDMP. Likewise, many of the respondents in the postgraduate survey commented that face-to-face interaction was needed for truly effective learning and that, while the available technologies could support collaboration, online MDMP was not beneficial.[7] The following are examples from the exit survey:

> I did not receive satisfactory learning value from the virtual classroom environment. The MDMP and other decision making processes are designed to be accomplished through a group dynamic. The synergy needed between the staff to be successful is difficult to accomplish via DCO, conference calls, and emails. I would recommend that the course offer a two week resident phase in one central location to cover portions of the O100 block and all of the O200 and O300 blocks of instruction. This would give the students the opportunity to work together in a staff environment.

> It was very hard to coordinate and get the full experience via e-mail and DCO.

> There really isn't much training value in doing an MDMP exercise and making plans for warfighting when everyone just meets online. It is not the same. Bringing everyone together at the end would enrich the exercise and we would learn more.

Although students reported being satisfied with peer feedback (see Figure 3.3), open-ended responses cited challenges to collaboration. A number of students reported that other team members were "free riders" and that there was no accountability and therefore no

---

[7] We surmise that the challenges of conducting MDMP in a distributed setting were due to the complex nature of the task rather than students' level of prior experience. MDMP is covered in the Captains Career Course and in the ILE Common Core, both of which are prerequisites for AOC. Furthermore, some students may have field experience using MDMP.

consequences for not pulling one's weight. Comments provided in the postgraduate survey echoed these points. For example,

> AOC was usually a few students of a group doing all the work, while the rest did not do anything, yet still received a grade.
>
> Additionally not offering this course in a controlled (classroom) environment makes it easy for the student body to place ILE-AOC second to other life's demands, thus cheat[ing] the entire class of the learning process.

The second quotation illustrates that free riding was problematic not only because it put an unfair burden on teammates but because it interfered with opportunities to learn from others, which is an important aspect of the course design. Respondents to both surveys recommended using peer evaluations to increase accountability.

Other comments reflected difficulties coordinating team efforts due to geographic/time dispersion, creating additional access issues. Several students recommended forming staff groups among students in the same time zones. For example,

> The collaborative blocks need to be conducted in the resident phase. Very difficult to manage when classmates are scattered across several time zones.
>
> [I]f there is a way to have students in the same time zones placed into groups it would enhance the ability of the class to communicate. A challenge and problem that our class had was the multiple time zones that students had without understanding the amount of work and communication that was needed to ensure that the group was able to work as a staff effectively.

Specific Technologies, Especially Defense Connect Online, Interfered with Learning Processes for Some

Whereas some students were satisfied with DCO sessions or wanted more, a number of students noted functional or reliability problems with the medium:

> DCO and MDMP, in my opinion, do not mix.
>
> DCO is nice for a conference call or even a brief but online collaboration is a joke. Only one person can effectively talk at a time, side bar conversations which facilitate learning and sharing of ideas, are nearly impossible.
>
> Better system for DCO. Often did not work or worked poorly and was often a distraction.

These responses to the open-ended questions provide a rich source of data about students' experiences. However, answering open-ended questions (on the part of students) and analyzing them (on the part of staff) is time consuming, and some of these aspects of the course can be measured with closed-ended questions. Thus, we explored issues of collaboration and technology in more depth in the postgraduate survey using a number of closed-ended questions.[8] We also added questions to measure student characteristics that came up as obstacles to working on the course, i.e., conflicting work and family commitments and motivation for the course.

Students Had More Favorable Responses Regarding Instructor-Student Interaction than Student-Student Collaboration

First, we asked graduates to indicate which technologies they used for collaboration in AOC-BDL. Results are shown in Figure 3.14.

We followed this question with items asking students to rate the degree to which collaborative learning activities (DCO sessions with instructors, threaded discussions, and DCO sessions with peers) contributed meaningfully to course objectives. Other questions about process asked about free riding (whether team members pulled their weight), and ease of scheduling group collaborative sessions, and we included a question about the adequacy of training on how to use course collaborative technologies. These items were rated on six-point agree/disagree scales.

---

[8] We also provided respondents with an opportunity to share their comments about these learning processes, but systematic analysis of these responses was beyond the scope of this report.

Figure 3.14
Type of Collaborative Technologies Used in Advanced Operations Course Blended Distributed Learning—Postgraduate Survey

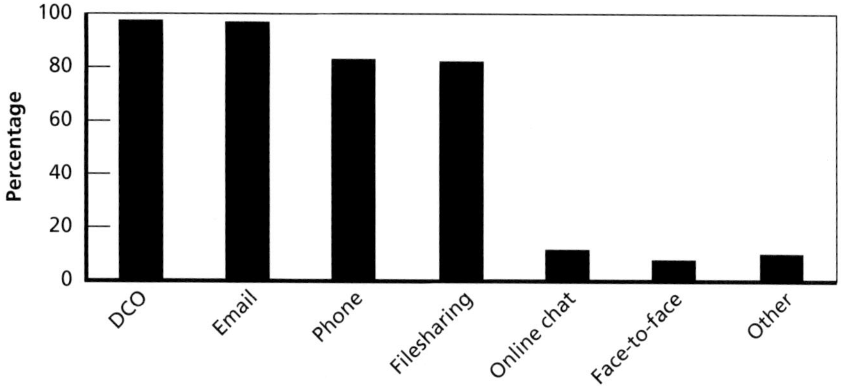

NOTE: Filesharing included Blackboard, Army Knowledge Online, and Google Docs. Some students used more than one filesharing application. "Other" included Skype, wikis, blogs, text, and social media.
RAND *RR172-A-3.14*

Responses are shown in Figure 3.15. Mean ratings ranged from 3.03 to 4.74 (out of 6). In general, responses tended to be more favorable for aspects of the course involving instructor-student interaction (the three bars on the left in Figure 3.15) than for aspects of the course that rely on student-student collaboration (the three bars on the right). Responses indicate that free riding and scheduling group sessions were problematic. Students found it especially difficult to schedule collaborative sessions with their groups.

Inputs

Reliability of Technology Posed Problems for Some Students

In addition to addressing the quality of technology-mediated collaboration, we asked graduates whether technology reliability and access to computers presented obstacles to working on the course.[9] Figure 3.16

[9] Future research is needed to determine whether technology was a greater obstacle for those who did not finish the course.

Figure 3.15
Ratings of Collaborative Learning Processes and Technology—Postgraduate Survey

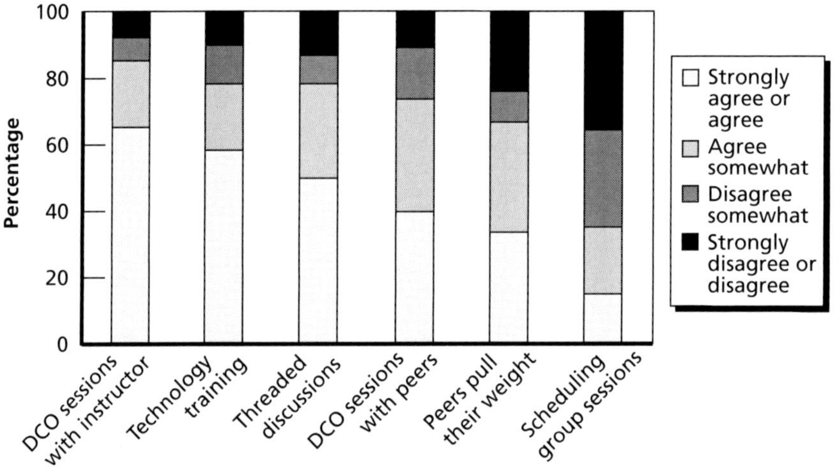

RAND *RR172-A-3.15*

Figure 3.16
Technology Reliability and Access as Obstacles to Advanced Operations Course Blended Distributed Learning—Postgraduate Survey

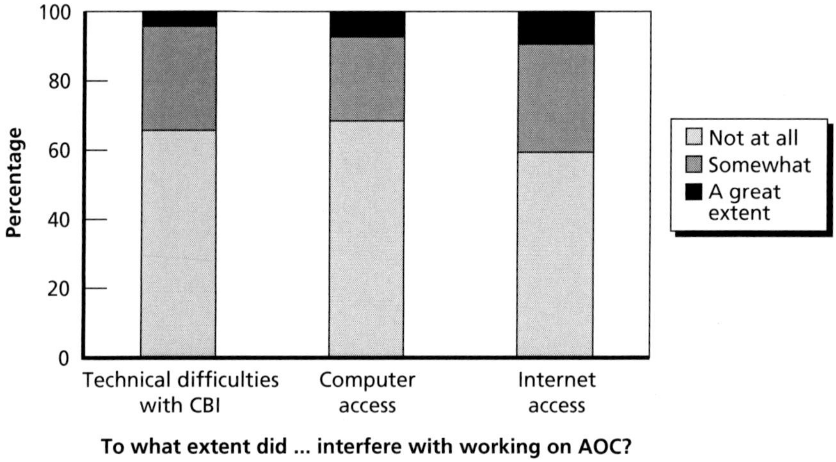

RAND *RR172-A-3.16*

shows responses to questions about technical difficulties with CBI, reliable computer access, and reliable Internet access. Approximately 30 to 40 percent of students had problems with one or more of these issues. We also asked students where they were located when they took the course. Not surprisingly, technical issues, such as Internet access, were more problematic among students who were OCONUS during part or all of the course (see Figure 3.17). Similar questions using yes-or-no options in the exit survey (not presented in the figure) showed that 13 to 23 percent of respondents had trouble accessing a reliable computer; playing audio, video, or animations; or accessing the course over the Internet. CGSS staff also reported that technical problems with DCO and Blackboard were common.

Student Characteristics May Constrain Participation or Engagement in Advanced Operations Course Blended Distributed Learning

Students appeared to be putting in substantial time working on AOC; over 50 percent of the graduates reported spending nine hours or more per week on AOC-BDL (see Figure 3.18). However, students reported

Figure 3.17
Internet Access Issues Based on Student Location During the Advanced Operations Course—Postgraduate Survey

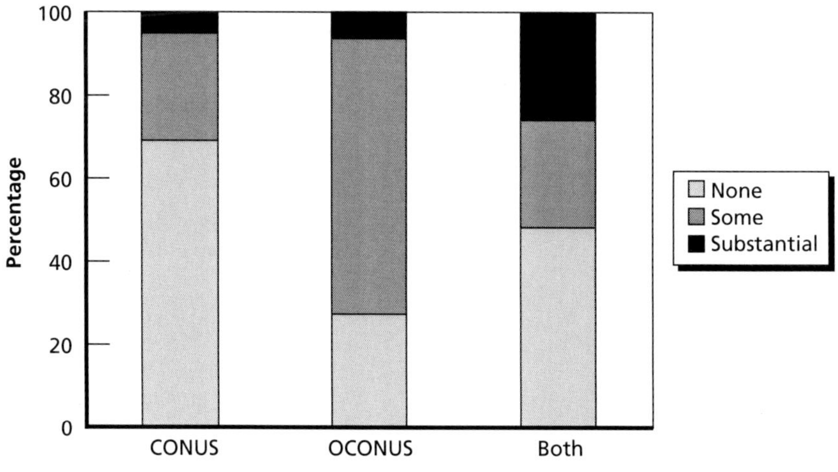

RAND *RR172-A-3.17*

Figure 3.18
Hours per Week and Payment Status—Exit and Postgraduate Surveys

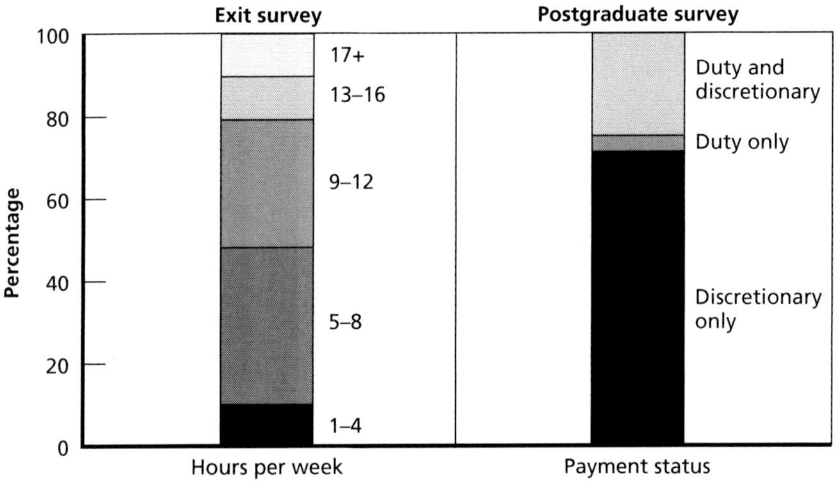

RAND *RR172-A-3.18*

several obstacles to working on the course. As described in Chapter Two, students have substantial family and work commitments, and students' responses to open-ended questions reported earlier in this chapter indicated that these commitments often interfered with spending time on AOC-BDL.[10] Data from the exit survey showed that the majority of students were working on discretionary time.

Because work and family status information was collected in the entrance survey, and survey responses could not be matched across surveys due to anonymous data collection, we could not analyze the association of work and family commitments and course outcomes in the exit survey. Therefore, we included a question in the postgraduate survey regarding the degree to which work and family commitments presented an obstacle to working on the course. As shown in Figure 3.19, only 14 percent of students reported that work and family commitments *did not* interfere with working on the course.

[10] Future research is needed to address the question of the extent to which family and work commitments explain students' decisions to drop out of the course.

Figure 3.19
Work and Family Commitments as Obstacles to Advanced Operations Course Blended Distributed Learning—Postgraduate Survey

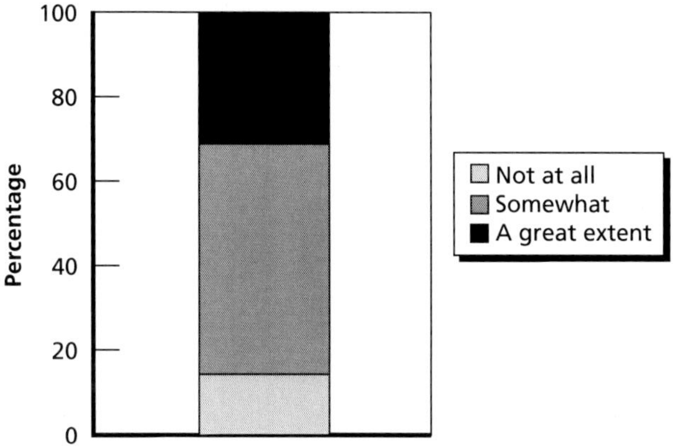

RAND *RR172-A-3.19*

We also examined students' motivations for training or learning to understand their reasons for taking AOC and how these might influence the amount of effort they exert in the course and their willingness to recommend the course to others. In response to a question asking graduates to rank their reasons for taking AOC-BDL, most students reported extrinsic sources of motivation; 58 percent reported that their primary motivation was promotion, and 9 percent reported other reasons, such as taking the BDL course because they were told to do so or to avoid moving their families to Fort Leavenworth to take the resident course. Approximately one-third of the students said that their primary reason was to improve their performance or professionalism. Thus, only one-third of the students reported that an intrinsic motivation was the primary motivation. There was a modest association between motivation (intrinsic or extrinsic) and the amount of time that students reported working on the course, with students who were intrinsically motivated reporting that they spent more time on the course ($\chi^2_{(3)} = 7.13, p = 0.06$). The association of motivation with course outcomes is reported next.

Putting It All Together: Inputs, Processes, and Outcomes

Peer collaboration, interaction with instructor, and student motivation were most strongly associated with course outcomes. We conducted a series of analyses to examine associations among inputs, processes, and outcomes. In the exit survey, we examined whether student input variables, i.e., demographic and background characteristics, including rank, payment status while taking the course (i.e., on personal time, paid time, or a combination), and year of course completion, were associated with their satisfaction or ratings of learning effectiveness. There were few or no differences in ratings of outcomes based on these student characteristics.

In the postgraduate survey, we conducted a series of hierarchical regression analyses to examine the association of student characteristics (inputs) with overall student satisfaction and perceptions of learning effectiveness in critical field-grade skills (outcomes). In addition, we examined the extent to which learning processes mediated (explained) the effect of these inputs on outcomes. A summary of results is reported in Table 3.4. In Step 1, student characteristics and technology reliability were entered into the equation for each outcome. In Step 2, measures of peer and instructor collaboration were added to the model to examine the extent to which these processes mediated the effect of inputs on outcomes. Asterisks indicate the statistical significance of each predictor. Significant coefficients for the mediator variables, in addition to a drop in significance for input variables, indicate that collaborative processes mediated or accounted for the effect of inputs on outcomes.

Results in Table 3.4 show the following:

- Technology reliability was not associated with outcomes.
- Time since graduation, which was included as a control variable, had a modest, positive effect on overall satisfaction after adding the process variables in Step 2. Inclusion of time since graduation did not affect results for any other variables in the model.
- Motivation was associated with overall satisfaction and perceptions of learning effectiveness (critical field-grade competencies).

Table 3.4
Results of Hierarchical Regression Analyses of Selected Outcomes

	Outcome			
	Overall Satisfaction		Critical Field-Grade Skills	
Predictor	**Step 1**	**Step 2**	**Step 1**	**Step 2**
Motivation	***	**	***	**
Time since graduation	ns	†	ns	ns
Technology reliability	ns	ns	ns	ns
Work and family commitments	*	ns	ns	ns
Collaboration and interaction processes; DCO sessions with peers		***		***
Team members pull weight		ns		ns
Scheduling collaborative sessions		ns		ns
Instructor interaction		***		†
Adjusted R^2	0.22***	0.56***	0.14***	0.31***
ΔR^2		***		***

NOTES: For postgraduates, overall satisfaction included the question asking whether respondents would recommend the course to others. †$p < 0.10$, *$p < 0.05$, **$p < 0.01$, ***$p < 0.001$.

Graduates who took AOC-BDL to improve their performance or professionalism were more satisfied and reported greater learning than did those who took the course for promotion or another reason (e.g., to avoid moving or because they were told it was required). The association of motivation with the outcomes dropped after inclusion of the process variables but remained statistically significant.

- Work and family commitments were negatively associated with overall satisfaction but were not associated with learning effectiveness. The effect for work and family commitments on overall satisfaction was not significant after including the process variables, indicating that learning processes fully mediated the relation-

ship between this input and outcome. That is, the effect of work and family commitments on overall satisfaction can be explained by the effect of work and family commitments on collaborative learning processes, which in turn affect satisfaction.
- Collaborative processes explained a substantial portion of outcome ratings beyond the input variables (motivation, technology reliability, and work and family commitments).

Conclusion

Responses to student surveys point to the need for improvements in course design and delivery and in survey design for subsequent evaluations. Results indicate that students were satisfied with the AOC-BDL overall and felt that it was meeting its core purpose. Nonetheless, when asked at the end of the course, 50 percent of the students reported that they would not recommend AOC-BDL to others (despite reporting that the course met its core purpose), and many respondents both at the end of the course and postgraduation reported minimal improvement in critical field-grade skills. Of particular note is the finding that graduates, in particular, had low ratings of critical skill development after returning to their units.

Although student self-reports can be correlated with learning outcomes (Alliger et al., 1997; Sitzmann et al., 2008), it is important to note that self-reported knowledge is not an objective measure of learning effectiveness. In Chapter Five, we discuss alternative measures of learning effectiveness and present different methods of evaluation for consideration. We also present a revised exit survey based on what we learned from responses to both the exit and postgraduate surveys.

Student comments and responses to questions in the postgraduate survey also revealed that the collaboration processes often detracted from learning. Findings indicate that a number of input factors, in combination, account for these results. In short, course objectives (focused on complex skills), course structure (completely distributed), technology (e.g., DCO capabilities; technology reliability), and student characteristics (e.g., employment and family status) appear to be interacting in ways that inhibit important learning processes. We explore these conflicts in more depth in Chapter Five and use the results of the literature review and case studies described in Chapter Four to propose options for modifications to the course.

CHAPTER FOUR

Literature Review and Case Studies of Blended Distributed Learning

In this chapter, we describe what we culled from the BL and DL literatures and from case studies in higher education (civilian and military) and industry. Our goal was to identify useful options for AOC based on best practices for BDL. We focused our analysis on practices that have documented support and would address major findings from the AOC-BDL survey data so as to directly contribute to options for improvement in the course. Despite an expansive literature on DL and BL, less has been written about the combination of BL and DL—BDL. Therefore, we have supplemented the literature review with case studies, including three original case studies conducted for this project and previously published case studies, where appropriate.

This chapter is organized according to the framework for online learning described in the introduction to this report. We describe six major findings, which align with outcomes, inputs, and learning processes, as shown in Table 4.1.

Literature Review Approach

The literature review focused on empirical studies of BDL. Given that completely DL is uncommon, we began our search using a variety of related terms, including "blended learning," "distributed learning + collaborative," and synonyms for DL, such as "distance learning" and "distance education." We searched in the following databases:

Table 4.1
Major Findings from Literature Review and Case Studies

Model Component	Major Findings
Outcomes	There is no clear advantage for resident instruction or BL, but there are few examples of effective all distributed BDL. However, research on virtual teams can fill some gaps in understanding collaboration at a distance.
Inputs	Instructional design, not the venue, is the key determinant of effectiveness, but successful BL and residential learning (RL) will have different designs.
	New technologies and instructional modalities require support to be effectively adopted for complex learning.
	Successful programs find ways to reduce conflicts with students' other commitments.
Learning processes	Virtual and collocated groups can achieve comparable outcomes, but differences in virtual team processes pose constraints for collaboration on complex tasks in BDL.
	Successful programs use a variety of methods to engage students in virtual interactive activities.

Psychinfo, PsychArticles, ERIC, Web of Science, JSTOR, and Google Scholar.

Searches were limited by the following criteria:

- source type: peer-reviewed journal, articles or books or reports (no dissertations)
- population: adult human subjects
- type of study: empirical
- date: 2007–2012
- language: English.

We especially looked for meta-analyses or sources with robust sample sizes. Once we identified a list of promising sources, we used "forward searching" (aka "snowballing") to identify similar sources. We also reviewed studies recommended to us by experts in the U.S. Army Training and Doctrine Command and other institutions, as well as seminal articles published before 2007. We also used experts to identify relevant research from the literature on virtual teams.

The results of our searches produced an initially large literature to examine. In the first pass, we identified over 1,600 potentially relevant sources based on article titles. We manually searched titles and abstracts to cull this list to 200 relevant reports using the following criteria:

- The study had to be quantitative and empirical, as opposed to descriptive or anecdotal.
- The study had to approximate the type of BDL that CGSS was using; thus, cases had to have no or limited face-to-face modalities and had to include some collaborative activities in the mix.
- The course studied had to deal with relatively high levels of learning and had to involve complex decisionmaking or critical thinking skills.
- Journals were restricted to those that dealt regularly with education or group collaboration.

For the third pass, we reviewed the articles themselves, applying the same criteria listed above as well as additional criteria relevant to robustness of the study methodology. For example, if we could not tell what modalities or technologies were used, there was no comparison group, the sample size was too small, or there were other significant threats to internal validity, we excluded the report from our analysis. This step reduced the number of relevant documents to about 25.

Case Study Approach

The purpose of the case studies was to identify best practices in BDL across different types of education and training settings. Therefore, we conducted an original case study in each of three settings: civilian higher education, military education, and industry. We searched for programs that had similar goals and served similar populations as AOC-BDL. Specifically, we looked for BDL or DL programs that served adult learners beyond the undergraduate level, used a variety of instructional modalities and media, incorporated collaborative activities (especially if done synchronously online), and had complex content and methods to teach learners how to apply critical thinking and leadership skills. We supplemented our three original case studies with published case studies when appropriate. We used similar criteria for selecting both original and published case studies.

Our search strategy included both online searches and consultations with experts. We used search engines (e.g., Google), combining learning environment terms (e.g., "blended learning," "distributed learning," "distributed blended learning," "distance learning") with organization types (e.g., "higher education," "college," "military [or a specific military service]," "industry," "organization," "company"). We explored websites of U.S. education associations, particularly those with a focus on online education (e.g., the U.S. Distance Learning Association and the Sloan Foundation). We also consulted with experts and looked for associations with awards for online education and training programs (e.g., the 2011 Brandon Hall Excellence in Learning Awards).

We selected the organizations and institutions shown in Table 4.2 for our original case studies, and we interviewed one or more program directors, staff members, and/or instructors at each site:

- Xerox: a recent leader of the Service Delivery eXcellence (SDX) program[1]
- Pennsylvania State University (PSU) World Campus: six World Campus directors and staff, two instructors in the online Master of Business Administration (MBA) program, one instructor of undergraduate and graduate turfgrass science and management courses, and one instructor of a master's degree course in educational leadership
- Naval Postgraduate School (NPS): two center directors, and one instructor in each of the following programs: Center for Homeland Defense and Security, executive MBA, human systems inte-

[1] Unlike our other case studies, the Xerox case involved an interview with only one expert. At the time of our interviews for the case studies, the Xerox SDX program was undergoing leadership changes, so we were able to access only one individual who had recently led the program.

Table 4.2
Case Study Site Descriptions

Type	Name	Program Features	Reason for Inclusion
Civilian Higher Education	PSU's World Campus	• Established in 1998 as online education division of PSU • Offers 80 degree or certificate programs • Serves 50,000 students worldwide[a]	• Experience and success in online education[b] • Size and diversity of programs • Programs include graduate degrees serving working-adult populations around the world • Programs focus on collaboration and teamwork and on management and leadership skills
Military Education	NPS	• Accredited graduate-level education and research institution run by the U.S. Navy • Offers resident and over 45 online degree and certificate programs to U.S. military personnel (mainly officers), government civilians, and federal contractors • Strong presence of international students • Average online enrollment for 2011 was 920 students, 65 percent of whom were civilian (personal communication from NPS, 2012)	• Diversity of online programs, serving working adults around the globe • Programs with learning goals involving critical-thinking, management, and leadership skills • Mix of online modalities and media listed by some of the programs
Industry	Xerox's SDX	• Designed for executives and managers • Teaches service delivery, how to solve service-related problems for clients and expand business opportunities • Six-month program is offered worldwide	• Course is long enough to warrant comparison to AOC-BDL • Focus on communication, problem-solving, and other leadership skills

[a] Not all 50,000 students earn online degrees—some are resident students taking online courses. Of the 50,000 in the World Campus, about 11,000 are students who take only online courses (i.e., through the World Campus).

[b] For example, the World Campus won two Sloan C-Awards in 2011: "John R. Bourne Outstanding Achievement Award in Online Education" and "Excellence in Institution-Wide Online Education."

gration, program management, and systems engineering. All programs except human systems integration, which was a master's-level certificate program, were master's degree programs.

Table 4.3 presents an overview of the case study programs.

Interviews were conducted in person or by phone between March and August 2012. We interviewed PSU World Campus directors and staff in person at the main PSU campus (State College, Pennsylvania) in March 2012. Interviews with PSU instructors were conducted by phone between May and June 2012. All NPS interviews were conducted in person at the NPS campus (Monterey, California) in June 2012. The Xerox interview was conducted by phone in August 2012.

Table 4.3
Overview of Programs/Courses in Original Case Studies

Org.	Program/Course	Year Started	Modality Mix	Student Characteristics
NPS	Executive MBA	2003	BDL/BL[a]	U.S. Navy aviators, government civilians
	Homeland Defense and Security	2003	BL[a]	U.S. government civilians in homeland defense
	Human Systems Integration	2009	DL	U.S. government civilians and contractors
	Program Management	2000	BDL	U.S. government civilians in acquisitions
	Systems Engineering	2000	BDL	Military officers, U.S. government civilians and contractors
PSU	Education Leadership[b]	2011	BDL	Kindergarten through Grade 12 educators
	iMBA	2002	BDL/BL[a]	Civilians, military officers
	Turfgrass Science and Management[b]	1998	DL	Senior undergraduates, graduate students
Xerox	SDX	2010	BDL	Service delivery executives and managers

[a] BL includes a face-to-face component.

[b] Information reflects courses, not entire programs.

We followed a semistructured interview protocol. Interviews with instructors were designed to solicit information about program or course structure, content, learning goals, resources, students (including quantity and characteristics), instructors, evaluations, instructional modalities, and media mix. For interviews with program or center directors and staff, the goal was to get a sense of institutional supports for DL programs, such as access to instructional designers and professional development for faculty new to DL instruction. Interview questions can be found in Appendix D.

Our case studies were not without limitations. First, as we have noted, not all programs were strictly BDL. For example, the human systems integration certificate program at NPS was completely asynchronous. Second, PSU and NPS learners self-select into programs, and there are differences between students who choose resident programs and those who choose DL programs. For example, NPS DL programs tend to have more civilians than military officers and vice versa for residential programs. Third, unlike AOC-BDL, the NPS and Xerox programs offer ways for students to complete coursework during work hours. We will come back to this point later in the chapter. Finally, it may be difficult to generalize from case studies, especially when there are few of them. We addressed some of these limitations by supplementing the original case studies with published case studies, which offered additional insights into instructional designs (e.g., small group activities) in BDL courses and reported outcomes (instructor and student feedback about the course). Published case studies include those described by Al-Busaidi and Al-Shihi (2012), Bisson et al. (2005), Bonk et al. (2002), and Park and Bonk (2007a, 2007b).

Findings from the Literature Review and the Case Studies

In the remainder of this chapter, we discuss in detail each of the six major findings listed in Table 4.1, drawing from both the literature review and case studies, as appropriate. As described above, findings are organized according to the framework for online learning described in the first chapter, first discussing outcomes, then inputs and learning processes.

Neither Resident Instruction nor Blended Learning Has a Clear Advantage, But There Are Few Examples of Effective All-Distributed Blended Distributed Learning

Although the present study does not compare AOC-BDL with AOC taught in residence, the BDL version of the course is modeled after the resident course and has many common features, including staff group size, online materials and reading assignments, collaborative sessions, and written assignments (see Chapter Two). Indeed, one goal of AOC-BDL course is to replicate the resident course. Therefore, we examined studies comparing resident instruction with BL or DL with an emphasis on collaboration.

Resident Instruction Versus BL and DL

Looked at broadly, there is a large, although inconclusive, research literature on how delivery medium influences effectiveness of training and education. Several studies have compared instructional media for adult learners (e.g., Phipps and Merisotis, 1999; Straus et al., 2006; Wisher et al., 1999) and have found no clear advantage for resident instruction or DL.

In a meta-analysis of 232 studies comparing DL and RL, Bernard et al. (2004) concluded that student achievement outcomes in DL compared to resident courses are extremely varied, with many DL courses outperforming their classroom counterparts, and many performing more poorly.

A series of studies that the Sloan Consortium sponsored rated DL as being as effective as residential instruction. For example, in a study of higher education (Allen and Seaman, 2011), 67 percent of academic leaders reported that online learning is as good as classroom instruction, although a large minority—33 percent—believe that online learning is inferior. In addition, according to Allen and Seaman (2011), results of a series of studies conducted over the eight years preceding their 2011 report found that learning outcomes for online education were as good as, or better than, outcomes from comparable face-to-face instruction.

More recent meta-analyses of studies comparing classroom and online learning for adult learners (Means et al., 2009; Sitzmann et al., 2006) also have concluded that DL has an advantage. Both of these studies found that, on average, students in online learning conditions performed better than those receiving face-to-face instruction. However, as in other reviews, many of the studies included in the meta-analyses had methodological weaknesses, such as selection biases, that could lead to erroneous conclusions. For example, in the Sitzmann et al. (2006) analysis, only a small number of studies were true experiments in which students were randomly assigned to training conditions. In these studies, the effects of medium were reversed, such that students performed better on tests of declarative knowledge in resident instruction than in DL.

Resident Instruction Versus Blended Distributed Learning

We found no robust large-scale studies that specifically compared BDL with face-to-face instruction or to BL. We believe there are a number of reasons for this gap in the research literature. First, many scholars may take for granted that face-to-face instruction needs to be part of the BL mix, at least when complex subjects are studied.[2] Second, accreditation organizations can push academic programs toward including face-to-face instruction. The interviewee from the executive MBA program at NPS indicated that business program accreditation does emphasize collaboration and that accreditation organizations tend to be more comfortable with face-to-face instruction than with online collaboration.

Third, a number of features of BDL (as well as of DL and BL) programs or courses make it difficult to draw conclusions about course format. For example, many educational programs (e.g., University of Phoenix) allow students to self-select into comparable online or residential courses, making random assignment of students to BDL and face-to-face courses impossible. This greatly increases the difficulty

---

[2] Furthermore, not all scholars consider it important to distinguish BDL from other modes of instruction. For example, Arbaugh (2008) looked at learning outcomes of 55 online MBA courses at a Midwestern U.S. university, some of which were BDL and some of which included face-to-face meetings, but the study did not examine whether outcomes differed depending on whether any face-to-face interaction occurred.

of making unbiased comparisons. In addition, BDL can be difficult to study because programs can vary widely within the same organization. At academic institutions like PSU and NPS, academic units (departments, schools) have authority over their instructors, who drive content and design. Instructors are not required to work with instructional design teams or to take professional development courses unless their units require them to do so. As a result, outcomes from multiple courses within a program are not easily aggregated, rendering results from large-scale program evaluations ambiguous.

Examples of Documented Blended Distributed Learning Success

Despite the dearth of research on BDL, we did find several examples of documented BDL success. These are discussed below.

Xerox Case Study

One example is the award-winning SDX program at Xerox,[3] one of our original case studies. The SDX program is designed to teach leadership skills to executives and managers around the globe. The program lasts six months, with classes meeting synchronously one to two times a month for a couple of hours using Adobe Connect. Asynchronous meetings among student groups (e.g., via a bulletin board space) occur in between, often focused on case studies that involve solving a client problem. In addition, students are expected to complete self-paced work and homework between sessions and to participate in individual coaching sessions with course facilitators. The course is evaluated via end-of-course and follow-up surveys. Findings from the surveys indicate training success as documented by learner satisfaction surveys administered right after the course and "impact surveys" given to both learners and their managers about a month and a half after the course.

---

[3] In 2012, Xerox won a "Learning Leader" award from Bersin and Associates, a research and advisory services firm specializing in enterprise learning and other areas of human resources and talent management. The goal of the competition was to find cases showing success combined with innovative approaches to enterprise learning in the corporate world. Among the reasons Xerox earned the award were technologies that were easy to use and access, strong instructional design (e.g., use of real-life scenarios and small group activities), buy-in from stakeholders at all levels, and a scalable solution. See Bersin et al., 2012.

In addition, the company determined in an internal study that the training had a positive return on investment.

Teaching Entrepreneurial Skills

Bisson et al. (2005) describes a successful pilot project to teach online entrepreneurship education among faculty and students at three universities in eastern Canada. Like AOC-BDL, this course was completely distributed (except that students could request face-to-face meetings with faculty at their local institutions) and used a diverse blend of synchronous and asynchronous online activities. Online activities included asynchronous CBI; an online business game; and three-hour synchronous sessions consisting of lectures, case study discussions, guest speakers, small group meetings, and workshops ("virtual labs").

Evaluation of the course relied on student feedback. Students generally had positive evaluations of many aspects of the course, including course relevance and usefulness, the amount learned, value of the case study approach, and instructor feedback. Instructional design, relevance to students' learning goals, and the extent to which the course met students' expectations received "above average" (defined as a rating of four on a five-point scale) ratings.[4] Students were enthusiastic about the virtual classroom technology and felt that it was an important aspect of the class. In response to 11 questions about the quality of instruction and the learning environment as compared to traditional, face-to-face instruction, in no case did the majority of students prefer traditional classroom instruction.

Teaching Professional Skills to Psychologists

Francescato et al. (2007) conducted a field experiment that compared the efficacy of collaborative learning among students randomly assigned to equivalent face-to-face and online university courses focused on developing professional skills and social capital for community psychologists in Italy. The face-to-face group completed its weekly collaboration and group exercises in a university classroom during a

---

[4] The aspects of the course that received lower ratings were those that were not necessarily related to the distributed nature of the course, such as course difficulty and usefulness of review exercises and quizzes.

three-hour period. The online group completed parallel work spread over the entire week using synchronous (e.g., chat for practice interviews) and asynchronous modalities (e.g., bulletin boards and email).[5] Analysis of student surveys and measures of learning outcomes showed that online students achieved or surpassed the face-to-face students in terms of growth in level of professional knowledge, social self-efficacy, self-efficacy for problem solving, and empowerment. Furthermore, a follow-up evaluation nine months after course completion showed that social ties, formed initially more in the face-to-face groups, lasted longer among online students.

Using Literature on Virtual Teams to Fill the Gap

Research comparing virtual and collocated teams can be used to fill some of the gaps in the BDL literature, particularly given the importance of collaboration in AOC. In brief, collocated teams typically outperform virtual teams on interdependent tasks and tend to have better social outcomes in the short term, but virtual teams tend to catch up over time. Nonetheless, there are differences in processes between virtual and collocated teams that have implications for learning in BDL. These findings are reviewed later in this chapter.

Instructional Design, Not Venue, Is the Key Determinant, but Successful Blended Learning and Residential Learning Will Have Different Designs

Importance of Instructional Design

Clark and Mayer (2011) argues that instructional methods, not the delivery medium, are the primary determinants of learning. Learning programs are effective when instructional strategies are designed to be compatible with human learning processes. Thus, DL and classroom education, for example, should show similar learning outcomes when each approach is designed to support psychological processes of learning (which we anticipate might be accomplished in somewhat different

---

[5] The online group did meet at the beginning and end of the course for administrative purposes and to complete surveys.

ways). We would add that each approach must use an instructional design that is suitable for the complexity of the material presented.

Good instructional design will often differ according to the delivery medium used. RL and DL designs can differ along many dimensions, including instructional approach, collaborative practices, feedback mechanisms, and grading strategies. Using the wrong design can affect learning outcomes. For example, Peters and Hewitt (2010) analyzed student survey and interview data and concluded that trying to emulate traditional classroom methods to determine "participation" grades in an asynchronous computer conferring course (e.g., by requiring a certain number of posts on an electronic bulletin board) can undermine rather than support learning. That is, in the online context, students would tend to adopt coping mechanisms that save time (e.g., skim rather than read other participants messages carefully) or that project an image of participation without advancing understanding.

A number of studies support the idea that appropriate instructional design depends on the medium. Bernard et al. (2004) verified the importance of instructional design principles in DL in a meta-analysis of the comparative classroom-distance education literature between 1985 and 2002. This study sought to explore what might be responsible for variability in findings across media, pedagogy (including instructional design),[6] course features, student demographics, and settings. In total, 232 studies were analyzed, covering the experiences of over 57,000 students. The results showed that the pedagogy used for the online course was a significant predictor of whether learning achievement was greater in the DL version of the course and was much more important than the particular media used.

More recently, Alonso, Manrique, and Vines (2009) conducted a field experiment in which 385 information technology specialists were randomly assigned to traditional classroom instruction, distance learn-

---

[6] Coded pedagogical features of courses included (among others) systematic instructional design procedures used, encouragement for student-teacher and student-student contact through activities or course design, and use of problem-based learning.

ing with virtualized course content,[7] or distance learning based on a proposed instructional model. The authors found that the residential version of a course was equivalent to the DL version only when the DL version used a specialized instructional model designed for e-learning.

In an online Delphi study of BL and CSCL (So and Bonk, 2010),[8] 20 educational experts from around the world gave their highest endorsement to the idea that design issues are paramount in BL and CSCL. Moreover, panel experts assigned highest importance to the statement that successfully fostering collaboration depends critically on how the course is designed to involve interaction with others. The authors concluded that getting the right mix of modalities and knowing when one type of interaction might substitute for another is an essential skill for BL course designers, requiring knowledge of how people learn and how they might successfully interact.

In a study of Army training, Tucker et al. also provided evidence of the need to adapt instructional strategies in BDL (Tucker, 2009). The authors conducted a study of two Force XXI Battle Command Brigade and Below classes for Army National Guard soldiers preparing to deploy. The course was designed to train digital skills remotely using BDL consisting of video teletraining and computer software. Using data from interviews and surveys of instructors and students and structured observations of classes, the authors identified a number of strategies that were especially effective for distributed learning, such as selecting capable students to model procedures, peer coaching, and conducting numerous brief practical exercises or checks on learning to reinforce key skills and facilitate problem-centered learning. The authors also concluded that instructors need to adjust their mix of training techniques to match the skill level of the students, which can vary from class to class.

---

[7] To create the course, materials from the residential course were simply converted to a digital format accessible via the Internet. The completely distributed course did not use a specific learning model or any additional instructional design.

[8] Part of the motivation for the study was the observation that, while learning technologies have been increasingly adopted, the focus appears to have been more on the delivery aspects of technology rather than on required pedagogical changes needed to successfully integrate technology in teaching.

Conole and Alevizou's 2010 synthesis of the research literature on the use of Web 2.0 tools in higher education provides other evidence of the importance of instructional design. Web 2.0 activities include instant messaging, chat and conversational arenas, social networking, blogging, wikis and other collaborative editing tools, online games, and virtual worlds. Despite the documented benefits of these technologies,[9] the authors noted the gap between the promise of the new technologies and their use in BL (and other areas).[10] The authors concluded that a lack of pedagogy for using these tools effectively contributes to this gap: In the absence of other guidance, practitioners tend simply to replicate face-to-face practices in an online context. Furthermore, when organizations introduce a new technology they tend to focus on its technical use at the expense of understanding how to use it effectively for learning (e.g., addressing how teaching must change to make effective use of that technology). Similarly, while funding for acquiring the technology is typically adequate, funding tends to be insufficient for activities to support successful uptake of the technology for instructional delivery (e.g., providing time for learning to use the technology in the course) and support when applying that technology to learning (e.g., providing students adequate means of addressing problems they encounter).

According to Conole and Alevizou (2010), some of the issues with pedagogy revolve around student attitudes and motivation. For example, in terms of student participation, there are concerns about student comfort in sharing their work and their willingness to complete "extra tasks" (e.g., participating in a social network) when the benefits are not clear. In terms of assessment, there are concerns with "unequal par-

---

[9] For example, wikis have been shown to foster active learning while facilitating creativity and socialization, leading to the development of higher-order cognitive skills. Social networking services have been shown to help bring informal knowledge building, mutual peer support, and discussions on shared interests to formal educational settings (see Conole and Alevizou, 2010).

[10] For other evidence of the underutilization of such technologies, see O'Neill, Scott, and Conboy, 2011. In that Delphi study, a group of instructors and CSCL experts tended to see newer technologies, such as multiuser environments, group conferencing, and social networks, as having limited usefulness.

ticipation, distrust in peer feedback and issues of ownership" (p. 66). Furthermore, even if students are sufficiently motivated, they may lack the skills to effectively participate. For example, Conole and Alevizou found that "learners need scaffolding, direction and modeling in the first instance, followed by practice and personalization, giving way to unstructured tasks through which they can learn to choose strategies and technologies to suit different situations and their own preferred ways of working" (p. 25). In total, what is needed is a fundamental transformation in the strategies used for designing, supporting, and assessing learning. Facilitating these kinds of changes, the authors concluded, will require expert guidance, as well as analysis and experimentation to challenge traditional teaching practices.

Need for Face-to-Face Interaction to Learn Complex Material

Although scholars have concluded that BL and RL require different instructional designs, many experts believe that effective BL dealing with complex material requires some degree of in-person instruction. Since early in the development of BL, many authors have suggested that including some face-to-face interaction may be a design feature required for maximum benefits of BL courses (e.g., Bernard et al., 2004). In fact, standard definitions of BL (which include some face-to-face instruction) and the scarcity of BDL programs and research may be an indication of the perceived need for some in-person instructional activities, particularly when teaching such skills as leadership.

Some evidence for this conclusion comes from another high-level Army course that used an experimental version of the Armor Captains Career Course (Bonk, et al., 2002). The course was designed to include three phases:

- an asynchronous IMI knowledge-based phase that each student completed individually (including instructor monitoring and feedback and equivalent to about 240 hours of residential instruction)
- a synchronous collaborative online phase that involved 10- to 12-person student groups acting as battalion staff officers who worked together to create, share, and evaluate tactical plans (con-

ducted on ten weekends and equivalent to about 60 hours of asynchronous and 120 hours of synchronous instruction)
- a two-week residential portion, including classroom sessions, simulations and field exercises, and a capstone experience in which students were challenged to apply what they learned in the first two phases.

In an evaluation of the course using student focus groups, Bonk et al. (2002) concluded that students felt that the most learning occurred in the residential portion of the course and that, in fact, the face-to-face portion was the phase where it "all came together" (p. 109).

In another context, a study examined outcomes from a course delivered exclusively online in environmental science at a university in Australia (Miller, 2007). Of particular interest were the students' views of the viability of wholly online learning. The 13-week course was specifically designed for DL and included collaborative portions that were conducted synchronously and asynchronous portions that were supported by video and audio material on a CD-ROM. Results from end-of-course surveys showed that, while many of the students recognized the benefits of the online portions, they preferred instruction that included at least some face-to-face components.

New Technologies and Instructional Modalities Require Support to Be Effectively Adopted for Complex Learning

As discussed above and in Conole and Alevizou (2010), slow uptake of Web 2.0 technologies in education may have limited the use of these tools in BL. However, the trend may not be that far from the norm. According to the technology adoption life cycle developed by Moore (2002), new technologies generally have a small group of initial "innovators," or people who try them out and/or experiment with them. If a technology shows promise and provides results, "early adopters" take it on and wait for an assessment of its viability. However, between the early adopters and the next group, the "early majority," there is a chasm or gap that must be filled with a critical mass of less technologically savvy users who are willing to commit to using the technology. Crossing this chasm places a large burden on developers to create usable systems and provide technical support for the early majority (Shanley et al., 2009).

User acceptance of technology is a critical factor associated with technology adoption in many domains (e.g., Venkatesh et al., 2003) and applies to technology uptake in education as well. Instructors are more likely to use a technology if they think it will improve student learning and will be easy to use (Hu, Clark, and Ma, 2003; Ma, Andersson, and Streith, 2005). Park and Bonk (2007a) argues that instructors need a variety of different types of support to accept and use new technologies. They recommend three types of support that institutions should offer instructors, as shown in the first column of Table 4.4. In the second column of Table 4.4, we provide examples of those types of support from different case studies.

As shown above, our original case studies offer examples of the first two types of supports that Park and Bonk (2007a) recommends. As an example of technological support, the Center for Educational Design, Development, and Distribution at NPS houses instructional

Table 4.4
Types of Support Needed to Help Instructors Accept New Technologies

Type of Support	Examples
Options for technologies to use for instruction and instructional design support	• The Center for Educational Design, Development, and Distribution at NPS houses instructional designers who work with faculty members to design and modify courses • Xerox SDX program has media producer to work with SMEs on PowerPoint presentations
Professional development for online instruction aimed at technology use and how to use technologies to support instructional design	• PSU's faculty development program offers courses for online teaching and, more recently, a certificate in online teaching • NPS offers professional development for faculty members
Incentives to take advantage of new technologies and to pursue professional development opportunities	• A few non-U.S. universities (e.g., Sultan Qaboos University in Oman) recognize online teaching and LMS use via awards, including promotions (Al-Busaidi and Al-Shihi, 2012; Schneckenberg, 2010)

SOURCE: Park and Bonk, 2007a.

designers who work directly with faculty members to design and modify courses. Our interview with the instructor for human systems integration highlighted the importance of the designer-instructor relationship. The instructor demonstrated some of the software that the designers customized for the program. Part of the customization plan was to make the software easy for instructors to modify (e.g., be able to add new content). PSU's World Campus provides similar instructional design support. One instructor who was new to online instruction indicated that working with an instructional designer helped her overcome her initial concerns that the online course did not have the same design as a residential course.

Xerox's SDX program also provided instructional design and technical support to SMEs who were asked to introduce cases to students in the online course. A media producer worked with the SMEs to make their PowerPoint presentations more interactive and visually appealing (e.g., adding graphics in place of text). The SDX program leader we interviewed stated that the producer met some resistance from the SMEs but was able to work through the issues.

Both NPS and PSU provide professional support for online teaching to all faculty members. For example, PSU's faculty development program has offered courses in online teaching since 2005. More recently, the program has moved toward offering a certificate in online teaching. The certification program will offer five core courses and several electives. The program is designed to improve faculty members' technical skills, teach them how to create effective instructional designs for online courses, and teach them how to engage students online (i.e., how to be "present"). At both NPS and PSU, faculty members are not required to take professional development courses to teach online unless their departments or programs require it. This speaks to Park and Bonk's (2007a) third recommendation about providing incentives for faculty members to use the supports. We are not aware of NPS, PSU, or Xerox using such incentives, and incentives to encourage instructors to teach online are not common in higher education institutions (Lion and Stark, 2010). However, recent studies suggest that faculty incentives can be effective for encouraging faculty to teach online. For example, in their survey of instructors' use of an LMS,

Al-Busaidi and Al-Shihi (2012) found that such incentives as recognition of online teaching in performance evaluations influenced instructors' satisfaction with the LMS and, in turn, their intentions to continue using the LMS.

In addition to these strategies to support instructors, our case studies revealed that commercial-off-the-shelf and open-source technologies can successfully support BDL courses. Interview participants cited a variety of such LMS technologies (e.g., Blackboard, Sakai, Moodle), synchronous collaboration (e.g., Adobe Connect, Elluminate *Live!*), nonsynchronous collaboration (e.g., SharePoint), and other nonsynchronous activities (e.g., YouSeeU). One NPS interviewee cited costs and freedom to customize as reasons for favoring open-source technologies. He argued that customizing a commercial off-the-shelf LMS can be costly; Blackboard, for example, requires more money for customizations. He believes that it is more cost-effective for NPS to customize on its own and rely on the community of users outside NPS to provide ideas and technical support.

However, customizing open-source software requires technological expertise. NPS is able to leverage open-source software because of its in-house expertise and because it operates in the dotedu domain. Most instructors do not have the skills or time to customize open-source technologies themselves. Open-source software also works best in nonrestrictive domains, such as dotedu. Despite being a military educational institution, NPS operates in the dotedu, rather than dotmil, domain because its faculty members cannot do all their research in a dotmil. Although NPS's concern about faculty research does not apply to CGSS, the security restrictions in a dotmil domain can limit use of off-the-shelf and open-source technologies for educational use.

Successful Programs Find Ways to Reduce Conflicts with Students' Other Commitments

An important finding from our case studies concerns how programs address conflicts with students' other commitments. As with AOC-BDL students, most of the students in the programs we studied are adults with work and family commitments. Moreover, students are geographically dispersed, making time-zone differences between students a challenge, especially for synchronous interactions. The programs address these challenges in two primary ways, as shown in Table 4.5.

As shown in the table, PSU programs preferred the first option. The World Campus directors and staff members we interviewed stated that they continue to use DL rather than move to BDL because their students would resist the restrictions on their time imposed by the need to participate in online synchronous sessions. When these faculty members do use online synchronous sessions, they do not mandate attendance and do not focus on new content (e.g., they use sessions for reviews or to discuss students' projects), and they record sessions for students who missed them. Instead, the World Campus tries to accommodate complex collaboration through more-common approaches to BL (i.e., using face-to-face interaction). This is exemplified by the online MBA program, which requires students to attend two one-week residencies to engage in complex collaborative teamwork.

NPS and Xerox SDX programs prefer the second option. As part of the enrollment process, NPS requires that organizations employing prospective students (e.g., a Navy command) agree to give students dedicated time for the course. For synchronous sessions, this arrangement can translate to a scheduled time each week (e.g., Fridays from

Table 4.5
Options for Addressing Challenges of Work/Family Commitments

Option	Examples
Limit online synchronous interactions	• PSU programs continue to use DL rather than move to BDL because of potential student resistance • Program tries to accommodate complex collaboration through more-common approaches to BL (i.e., using face-to-face interaction)
Engage students' employers to dedicate time for students' coursework	• NPS has requirement that students' employers agree to provide students with dedicated time for coursework • Xerox offers informational seminars to students' managers and updates them on students' progress • NPS and Xerox programs are tailored to specific career fields (e.g., acquisitions) or jobs (service delivery executives) relevant to employers • NPS and Xerox have more direct relationships with employers than CGSS can have with the employers of its AOC-BDL students

0800 to 1100 Pacific). Xerox SDX program leaders took a somewhat different approach to engaging students' employers. Because students and their managers are Xerox employees, the SDX leaders can engage directly with students' immediate managers. The program offers a seminar to orient managers to the program, including time commitments. Managers also receive user guides that summarize what their employees have learned and how they are progressing. If students change jobs within Xerox or otherwise get a new manager, the program works to get the new manager's commitment.

NPS and Xerox also offer employers two incentives intended to provide them direct value from student participation in courses. First, the NPS and Xerox programs are tailored to specific career fields (e.g., acquisitions) or jobs (service delivery executives). The knowledge and skills employees learn in these programs are intended to be directly relevant to work they do for their employers. Second, NPS and Xerox have more-direct relationships with employers than CGSS can have with the employers of its AOC-BDL students. NPS programs are sponsored by different organizations, who have influence over program design (i.e., act like accreditors). Even if an organization is not a sponsor, it may send several employees to the program. NPS programs will work with such organizations on scheduling, if need be. For Xerox SDX, the relationship is direct: Xerox students and employers are all Xerox (or Fuji Xerox) employees.

Virtual and Collocated Groups Can Achieve Comparable Outcomes, but Differences in Virtual Group Processes Pose Constraints for Students Collaborating at a Distance

While we do not present a comprehensive review of the abundant literature on virtual and collocated teams, we highlight some findings that have implications for collaboration and learning in AOC-BDL teams.

Performance Quality and Quantity

Studies that compare outcomes of collocated groups and technology-mediated teams show that collocated and virtual teams can achieve comparable performance quality but that virtual teams require much more time. In comparison to virtual groups using computer-mediated (text-based) communication, collocated teams perform better on interdependent tasks (e.g., decisionmaking, problem solving) in the short run (see Baltes et al., 2002). Collocated teams are more efficient and can complete more work in less time (e.g., Axtell, Fleck, and Turner, 2004). Similarly, collocated teams express more positive social outcomes, such as cohesion and trust, in the short term (e.g., Kiesler et al., 1985; Straus, 1997; Wilson, Straus, and McEvily, 2006). However, when time is not constrained (e.g., Baltes et al., 2002) or when virtual teams interact over time, they "catch up" to collocated teams in performance quality (e.g., Baltes et al., 2002; Hollingshead, McGrath, and O'Connor, 1993) and social outcomes (Walther, 1993; Wilson, Straus, and McEvily, 2006). Thus, virtual and collocated teams can achieve comparable outcomes, but it takes virtual teams much longer to do so.

Findings about the pace of communication have also been demonstrated in CSCL case studies. For example, the Bisson et al. (2005) study found that many of the synchronous sessions (which lasted three hours) could not cover all the material that was planned. Instructors argued that online verbal communications are "somewhat slower" in pace and "less fluid" than in-person verbal communications, thus making covering the same amount of content more difficult in online synchronous sessions (p. 53). Students' comfort with online synchronous communication and their ability to follow discussions were possible reasons for these issues; the authors found that students needed time to "warm up" to online synchronous interactions. Early on, some students argued that their participation grades should not be limited to participation in the synchronous sessions. As a result of this feedback, instructors allowed students to also use email for participation. However, as the course progressed, students increased their participation in the synchronous discussions and utilized asynchronous options less often.

Opportunities to Communicate and Develop Mutual Knowledge

Despite these positive outcomes for virtual teams, a variety of important processes in collocated teams are difficult to replicate in distributed groups. As reviewed by Axtell, Fleck, and Turner (2004), proximity, i.e., being in the same physical space, allows team members to be more aware of each other and of progress on group tasks. Proximity also facilitates initiating communication and conducting conversations (see Kraut et al., 2002), including chance encounters or "watercooler" conversations that enable members to discuss project work. In fact, most communication in work teams is opportunistic and occurs because seeing one's colleagues serves as a reminder of the need to communicate and an opportunity to do so (Armstrong and Cole, 2002; Kraut et al., 1990). Members of virtual teams may have a variety of information and communication technologies (ICTs) at their disposal, but some technologies require a planned effort to communicate and therefore do not overcome these barriers to spontaneous communication.

Although asynchronous communication has some benefits over synchronous interactions, such as enabling group members to compose their thoughts and providing an archive of their interactions, asynchronous and synchronous text-based communication present a number of other obstacles to effective team interaction, many of which occur due to an absence of nonverbal cues that help regulate discussion and convey meaning, a lack of immediate feedback, and disruptions in the sequence of contributions within discussion threads. As reviewed in numerous papers (such as Axtell, Fleck, and Turner, 2004; Griffith and Neale, 2001; and Hinds and Weisband, 2003), these features of technology result in misunderstandings or a lack of common ground, i.e., difficulty establishing mutual knowledge, including knowledge about content and other group members' expertise. In addition, when working at a distance, team members often are not aware of one another's context or situation. As a result, when a team member neglects to respond to a message or fails to keep a commitment, others may wrongly blame the individual rather than the context (Cramton, 2001; Cramton, Orvis, and Wilson, 2007).

Implications of Using Information and Communication Technologies for Learning

Straus and Olivera (2000) reported that, in comparison to face-to-face teams, members of virtual teams using computer-mediated (synchronous, text-based) communication had much less communication. Virtual teams also had less elaborate communication and were more likely to exchange information about "what" versus "how" or "why" when the latter types of interaction are particularly important for learning from others. Virtual team members also lack opportunities to observe team members, which is a factor that contributes to learning (e.g., Webb, 1992) and aids in the development of implicit knowledge (Nonaka, 1994). In a case study of distributed software development teams, Armstrong and Cole (2002) found that the inability to see successful project managers enact their roles disrupted opportunities for mentoring and learning by observation. Moreover, given the challenges of communicating at a distance, members of virtual teams may structure their work in such a way as to limit interdependencies (e.g., Galegher and Kraut, 1992; Straus and McGrath, 1994), thereby further restricting chances to learn from one another.

Successful Programs Use a Variety of Methods to Foster Student Engagement and Success in Online Interactive Activities

We looked to the case studies for instructional methods that could address some of the limitations of virtual groups described in the previous section. However, we broadened our scope to other forms of online interaction, not just those that require teamwork. Table 4.6 describes four methods intended to engage students to succeed in online interactive activities (both synchronous and asynchronous).

Training for Students

Just as instructors need support learning new technologies, so do students. While students might be familiar with the technology in other contexts (e.g., Facebook for personal use), this does not mean that they will see the value of using it to support learning in the course (Jones et al., 2010; Kvavik and Caruso, 2005). Park and Bonk's (2007a) analysis of a synchronous graduate-level course suggests that instructors should hold multiple practice sessions and establish rules and guidelines that lay out the instructor's expectations and the purpose and requirements for the interactive activities. For example, the Xerox SDX program had two or three introductory sessions by phone to introduce students to each other and teach them how to use the course technologies (e.g., web cams, Adobe Captivate).

Table 4.6
Methods to Engage Students to Succeed in Online Interactive Activities

Method	Examples
Instructor ensures students know how the technology for collaboration will be used	• Xerox SDX program had two or three introductory sessions by phone to introduce students to each other and teach them how to use course technologies (e.g., web cams, Adobe Captivate)
Instructor scaffolds discussions and provides timely feedback	• NPS Program Management Master's program instructor poses challenging questions in class and telephones students to pose questions to them
Small groups (two to six students) are used for interactive activities	• Students in PSU Turfgrass Science and Management program analyze three case studies and produce reports • Xerox SDX program uses case analysis activities in small groups of five to six students but does so synchronously
Peer evaluations are used to increase accountability for group activities	• Two instructors at NPS use peer evaluations to monitor whether there are students who are not contributing to their teamwork and to intervene if necessary • PSU's online MBA program has student teams develop contracts specifying rules about what members expect of each other and the consequences for not meeting expectations (e.g., missing a team meeting will cost you a dollar).

Instructor "Scaffolding" and Feedback

Instructor scaffolding and the provision of timely feedback have been found to be effective practices for online instruction (see Tallent-Runnels et al., 2006). An example from one of our original case studies comes from the program management master's degree program at NPS. The instructor we interviewed stated that, when discussions during synchronous sessions die down, he will pose a complex question and let it "hang out there" until students get uncomfortable enough for someone to finally answer it. Another technique he uses to increase student participation during synchronous discussions is cold calling: He will call individual students on the phone and ask them questions. The instructor also indicated that he spends a lot of time (including nights and weekends) interacting with individual students or teams. He provides feedback during these meetings, as well as when students present products that will be graded. Students value such support: Park and

Bonk (2007b) found that graduate students in an educational technology course listed instructor scaffolding and timely feedback among the helpful instructional strategies offered during synchronous class sessions. As described in Chapter Three of this report, student-instructor interaction was one of the most favorably viewed aspects of AOC-BDL.

Use of Small Groups

Another helpful instructional method identified by students in the Park and Bonk (2007a, 2007b) case study was the use of small groups. The authors reported that instructors also felt that small groups (three students) were useful for synchronous sessions. Our original case studies also revealed the common use of small groups (two to six students) for online interactive activities (both synchronous and asynchronous). An instructor in PSU's turfgrass science and management programs provided an example of an asynchronous interactive activity he uses in one of his courses. Students analyze three case studies and produce reports following course guidelines. Although students analyze their own cases, they also interact in five- to six-person teams to critique each other's reports. They are required to ask two specific types of questions about each of their teammates' reports in a team discussion forum (similar to the threaded discussions used in AOC-BDL). The instructor monitors team discussions and will scaffold discussions (e.g., model how to ask probing questions) as needed. The Xerox SDX program also uses case analysis activities in small groups of five to six students but does so synchronously. During synchronous sessions, students use breakout rooms in Adobe Connect (an online synchronous tool) to interact with their teammates. The team has to jointly develop a solution to a service problem of a hypothetical client. The instructor monitors teams and facilitates as necessary.

Peer Evaluations

In addition to the instructional methods above, peer evaluations were also mentioned in our case studies (and were suggested by AOC-BDL graduates in both the exit and postgraduate surveys). The purpose of peer evaluations is to keep teammates accountable for contributing to group efforts. Two instructors at NPS indicated that they use peer evaluations to monitor whether there are students who are not contributing to their teams and to intervene if necessary (which suggests that peer evaluations are ongoing and are not solicited only at the end of the course).

Other methods for student accountability were also described in the case studies. For example, PSU's online MBA program has student teams develop contracts specifying rules about what members expect of each other and the consequences for not meeting expectations (e.g., missing a team meeting will cost you a dollar). A program advisor provides guidance to the teams—an instructor from the program likened this advisor to a "marriage counselor." Another accountability method was previously mentioned: requiring students to ask a certain number and type of questions during online discussions. Two of the three faculty members in PSU programs (turfgrass science and management and educational leadership) specifically mentioned this method.

Conclusion

Based on case studies and the BL and DL literature more broadly, this chapter describes six major findings related to best practices for BDL that potentially apply to AOC. These findings address outcomes, inputs, and learning processes for online courses, with a focus on courses for adult learners and with learning goals similar to those in AOC (e.g., involving complex skills and team collaboration).

Outcomes

The first finding is related to learning outcomes. From a review of empirical studies, we conclude that residential instruction has no clear advantage over BL. Furthermore, despite the dearth of research on BDL in general, we found several documented examples of its success.

Inputs

We identified three major findings related to course inputs. First, sound instructional design is key and is much more important than the venue in determining learning success. Good instructional design will often differ according to the delivery medium used, and, more particularly, DL requires its own specialized design. Many experts conclude that, to address complex material, effective BL design will require some degree of in-person instruction.

Second, successful BL and DL programs offer support to instructors to help them adopt new technologies and instructional modalities. Such support includes (1) a choice of technology options together with instructional design support, (2) professional development for online instruction, and (3) incentives to take advantage of new technologies.

Third, successful programs use a variety of approaches to mitigate conflicts in adult learners' busy lives. Some programs limit the use of online synchronous activities. Others actively engage students' employers to obtain dedicated time for student coursework.

Learning Processes

This chapter also described two major findings about learning processes. First, compared to collocated groups, virtual groups experience more hurdles to collaboration on complex tasks. For example, virtual groups require additional time to achieve outcomes comparable to those of collocated groups, and the lack of nonverbal cues can make it difficult for virtual team members to achieve common ground. Second, instructors in successful online programs use various approaches to engage students in online interactive activities, such as training students on collaborative technologies, using scaffolding during synchronous or asynchronous (e.g., threaded) online discussions, and limiting group size (to two to six students) when they want students to engage in complex collaborative activities. Finally, some instructors require students to evaluate their peers during group activities as a way to increase accountability.

These findings, in combination with the survey results discussed in Chapter Three, serve as a foundation for the conclusions and the discussion of options for improvement found in the final chapter.

CHAPTER FIVE

Conclusions and Options for Improvement

AOC develops key competencies in officers and uses DL (specifically, BDL), which is consistent with the goals of the Army Learning Model. To develop these competencies, AOC-BDL uses a more ambitious approach than most standard DL or BL in the Army or elsewhere in that it requires substantial instructor-student and student-student interaction and is completely distributed and often synchronous.

In this chapter, we summarize our conclusions and then list various options for improvement. Both were informed and shaped by our findings about AOC-BDL (in Chapter Three) and by our findings from the literature review and the case studies (in Chapter Four). In addition, we provide recommendations for revisions to the exit survey used in AOC-BDL (see Appendix B) and for conducting more-comprehensive evaluation of the course.

Conclusions

AOL-BDL Has a Number of Strengths

Developing and teaching a course involving collaborative staff planning skills to distributed students working on discretionary time is a complex endeavor, and results show that CGSS's DDE is successful in many respects. Analysis of student survey responses showed that most students (nearly 80 percent) report that AOC-BDL meets its core purpose. Furthermore, students give high ratings to items about the importance of student-instructor and student-student interaction, and students are consistently satisfied with their instructors. Students also report that most CBI lessons are effective. These indicators of success are more impressive in light of the fact that many students do not have a choice about the medium; that is, they cannot elect to attend the resident course or the BDL course. In contrast, many educational institutions offer students a choice: Students self-select into resident or DL instruction. As a result, the relative effectiveness of resident and DL instruction is often difficult to determine. Thus, AOC provides a "cleaner test" with respect to understanding the quality of the course. CGSS's continuous improvement process for AOC-BDL is yet another strength of the course in that it gives the school opportunities to identify and make needed adjustments.

In addition to these strengths, participation in AOC-BDL provides some benefits that students in the resident course do not experience. Notably, by collaborating in virtual teams on complex tasks, students in AOC-BDL learn to work in situations that are increasingly common in operational environments and in other institutional settings (Alberts and Hayes, 2003). In addition, although geographic and temporal dispersion in teams is frequently disruptive to teams, groups can sometimes benefit by working across time zones because members can hand off work to one another (Colazo, 2010).

Improvements Can Be Made

Despite significant constraints, most students think AOC-BDL meets its overall goals. However, given the difficulty of executing the course in this environment, it is not surprising that there are some needs for improvement. Table 5.1 summarizes key objectives in AOC and issues or areas for further investigation and/or improvement identified in this study.

With respect to operational planning, findings that a number of students felt unprepared to serve as field-grade commanders or staff officers in interagency and multinational settings may not be surprising, given that AOC focuses on operational levels, while the Common Core focuses on strategic levels. CGSS staff also noted that many staff groups in AOC-BDL lack international or interagency students. At the same time, it is important to consider that part of the complexity of current operations is that brigade, division, and combined forces land

Table 5.1
Key AOC Objectives and Needs for Improvement

Key AOC Objective	Issue/Area for Improvement
Operational planning	Low ratings of ability to work in interagency and multinational environments
Developing critical field-grade skills	Many students, particularly graduates, do not see benefit
Staff group collaboration	Students saw issues with effective collaboration at a distance, particularly in planning and executing MDMP

component command operations occur, and will continue to occur, in a multinational and interagency environment. This suggests that such activities as role-playing exercises should reflect the complexity of actual operational environments and that the curriculum should not rely on members of student staff groups to provide this expertise.

One possible explanation for low ratings of perceived learning effectiveness, particularly with respect to abstract competencies, such as critical thinking, is that students do not know what they know (or what they do not know). Even if this is the case, we think that the scores were low enough to warrant a reexamination of multiple areas of learning effectiveness. For example, it would be beneficial to obtain input from students' commanders before and after the course with respect to knowledge, skills, and abilities in these areas. Responses could point to the need for improvements in course design, instructional methods, or course content and in mechanisms for demonstrating learning to the students themselves.

Tensions Among Key Aspects of AOL-BDL Mean That Equivalence with Resident AOC Is Not Feasible

AOC-BDL is a demanding, broad, and complex course that requires substantial time commitments for both in-class and out-of-class activities. Collaboration that fosters deep learning is a clear requirement for effectiveness. Furthermore, the required collaboration must be accomplished entirely with students who are distributed. Collaboration among diverse teams becomes particularly challenging when students are widely distributed across time zones and rely on ICTs for group work, since technology-mediated communication increases the time it takes for students to accomplish the required tasks. This is particularly true on DoD networks, which can impose significant restrictions affecting technology reliability and functionality. Moreover, because a sizable proportion of students are taking AOC-BDL to fulfill a requirement (a proportion that will increase with the surge in throughput of students in the course), many students may lack intrinsic motivation. In addition, the students who take this course have substantial constraints in the form of job and family responsibilities and are working largely on discretionary time. Thus, the students who have perhaps the least amount of time available are being asked to collaborate using some of the most time-consuming methods.

In short, the course is characterized by factors that are in conflict with each other. Results suggest that these factors impede collaboration and other learning processes and ultimately lead to negative associations with student satisfaction and learning effectiveness. We thus conclude that AOC-BDL is not equivalent to the resident course, a finding that is substantiated by students' comparisons of AOC-BDL with their experience in the Common Core. Given the instructional approach in combination with student and technology constraints, we conclude also that equivalence is not feasible. However, equivalence may not be the primary goal. If so, the question for CGSS then becomes whether the current outcomes are good enough, and if they are not, what changes are both desirable and attainable.

Decisions Are Needed Regarding the Composition and Role of Distributed Teams

Based on the data presented, we see the greatest need for improvements in the area of collaboration to support teamwork and learning processes, particularly given the strong association of collaborative processes and outcomes reported in Chapter Three. If the goal is to improve course design and delivery with respect to these processes, it is particularly important to take note of findings from the literature and case studies regarding the need for different designs in DL and RL.

The primary questions that need to be asked include the following:

- Should the course content for distributed teams focus on depth or breadth of coverage?
- What alternative media and methods best support course goals in general and virtual teams in particular?
- In what other ways can collaborative processes be improved?
- How can the family and work constraints influencing distributed collaboration be reduced?

While answering the first of these questions is beyond the scope of the present study, our options for improvement address multiple aspects of the remaining questions.

Options for Improving Course Design and Delivery

We present a number of options for improvement in course design and delivery, focusing on different sets of course inputs or strategies. These alternatives are not mutually exclusive; in fact, we expect that several of the options will be needed. Table 5.2 presents a summary of the proposed options.

Change Course Design to Complement Collaborative Technology Capabilities and Student Characteristics

Add a resident segment. Adding a resident segment to the class, e.g., a one- to two-week period at the end of the course in which students work on the most intensive collaborative activities, such as OPORDs, offers the greatest potential for improvement. This suggestion is based on student evaluations of the course in combination with best practices identified in our case studies—such as PSU, which continues to use DL or, when complex collaboration is needed, uses BL with a residential component. Of course, adding a residential segment to AOC-BDL is also the most complicated option in terms of scheduling and resourcing. Indeed, this option may not be feasible due to available infrastructure, costs, and operational manning requirements associated with TDY and course staffing. In addition, the Army has limited capacity to take officers away from their functional duty assignments for extended

Table 5.2
Summary of Options to Improve Course Design and Delivery

Strategy	Suggestion
Change course design	Add a one- to two-week residential segment at the end of the course to work on the most intensive collaborative activities
	Shift some of the collaborative activities to higher level IMI or other assignments with iterative student-instructor interaction; have fewer but more in-depth synchronous exercises
	Implement peer evaluations
	Offer additional instructor facilitation to student groups
	Provide training in team facilitation skills
Change composition of student groups	Use smaller groups for team assignments, as well as for larger exercises, such as creating OPORDs
	Compose groups based on time zone
Affect organizational policy	Encourage chain of command or employers to provide dedicated time for training
Change technology to fit course design	Move to a dotcom or dotedu domain
	Pilot alternative technologies for group collaboration and group online gaming/simulations

periods without having a negative mission impact. In light of these constraints, we argue that the remaining strategies become particularly important to consider.

Shift some of the collaborative activities to higher-level IMI or other in-depth individual assignments; have fewer but more in-depth synchronous exercises. For this option, we suggest making greater use of IMI, which the students generally viewed favorably. Here, we suggest shifting some of the collaborative activities to a relatively high-level IMI (e.g., Level 3) and having fewer but more in-depth synchronous exercises, with more time spent reviewing plans, discussing the rationale for students' decisions, and evaluating alternative courses of action.[1] While greater use of IMI might free some instructional resources, it also can be costly to develop and maintain. Alternatively, students could be given in-depth individual assignments with iterative student-instructor interaction to foster complex thinking skills.

Increase accountability through peer evaluations, additional or optional facilitation by instructors, and training students in team facilitation. One strategy for increasing accountability in teams is to use peer evaluations or contracts, as noted in the NPS case study and as suggested by some students in the AOC-BDL exit surveys. In peer evaluations, team members typically are asked to rate other members of their team on several criteria on an anonymous basis. These ratings could contribute to course participation grades.

Better facilitation for student groups as they work on their assignments could also reduce free riding. This could be accomplished by having the instructor join in students' initial DCO work sessions to demonstrate effective facilitation and then hand off this responsibility to the group for subsequent meetings. To complement this approach, the instructor could train students to serve in structured meeting roles (e.g., facilitator, timekeeper, scribe; Kayser, 2010) with the expectation that students would alternate performing these roles during group sessions.

---

[1] DoD defined four levels of interactivity in IMI that reflect the type of interaction required of the learner (DoD, 1999). Level I IMI is passive, requiring minimal interaction with content (e.g., reading text, navigating forward and back, answering multiple choice questions). Level II involves limited interaction with content, such as drag-and-drop exercises, using interactive animations, or typing in a response to a question and comparing it to a standard. Most of the IMI in AOC is Level II. Level III requires more complex participation in which the learner can enter a variety of responses, and branching logic results in different consequences depending on the response. Level IV involves real-time interaction in lifelike simulations, allowing myriad scenarios and rapid feedback. Level IV IMI typically would be conducted in groups with a facilitator.

As CGSS begins to fill the backlog of students who need to complete AOC, the pool of students in the BDL course might be large enough to assign students to a staff group based on the echelon that is most relevant to them. This way, collaborative exercises could provide more depth by focusing on one echelon rather than three. In addition, this approach might enhance students' motivation for the course because it would develop skills that they could apply in the near term.

The suggestion to use such strategies as peer evaluation to alleviate free riding are relatively low (or no) cost. Training students to facilitate groups also complements goals of AOC more generally.

Change Composition of Student Groups

Use smaller groups for exercises. A second suggestion is to use small groups, not only for team assignments (which is current practice) but also for larger exercises, such as briefing courses of action. For example, using eight-person rather than 16-person groups would reduce free riding and alleviate some of the challenges of coordinating synchronous sessions and integrating work products. Smaller groups for instructor-led DCO sessions would also increase interaction between students and the instructor and allow more in-depth discussions, facilitating development of critical thinking, problem solving skills, and oral communication skills. Using small groups is a strategy used in many of the cases reported in Chapter Four.

Minimize temporal dispersion. Generally, instructors attempt to compose groups of students in the same (or close) time zones, but this may not be possible if students with expertise needed for a particular assignment are temporally distant. In addition, instructors have discretion in how they compose groups, and there may be variation in these practices across faculty members. CGSS should emphasize the importance of composing groups based on time zones and, if a particular area of expertise needed for a group assignment is not available in a close time zone, provide a "stand-in" (e.g., the instructor or another faculty member, using prepared role-based materials such as intelligence estimates). Opportunities to compose diverse teams of members from similar time zones should improve, given the substantial increase in throughput anticipated for AOC-BDL, as described in Chapter Two.

Affect Organizational Policy

Encourage employers to provide dedicated time for training. It may be possible to reduce conflicts with job commitments by engaging students' employers (including commanders). The recommendation follows the NPS practice in which employers commit to providing time for their employees to complete coursework. Implementing this recommendation would entail informing employers when an employee is taking the course, setting expectations about what the student is required to do, and asking for support to allow the student to spend time on the course. As one student in the exit survey suggested:

> Recommend to develop memorandum of understanding from schoolhouse to the student commander that will support ILE students to complete this requirement. This is a military requirement and a DOD school that should receive time from work to complete.

Although CGSS may not be able to provide employers (particularly outside the military) with direct incentives or involve them in program design (as Xerox does, for example), many of the skills addressed in AOC, such as problem solving, communication, and working on complex tasks in distributed teams, are relevant to a wide variety of jobs. Thus, CGSS might gain buy-in through efforts to inform employers about how they can benefit from their employee's participation in the course.

Change Technology to Fit Course Design

Moving the course to a dotcom domain could potentially alleviate some technology reliability issues that may inhibit access to the course. Hosting the course and related tools for collaboration in the dotcom or dotedu domain can also provide more options for collaborative technologies. For these reasons, CGSS is piloting use of Blackboard.com with some staff groups and anticipates moving to a dotcom domain entirely by 2014.[2]

A second suggestion is to continue to explore technologies. These include ICTs for collaboration that support student-instructor and student-student interaction, such as those reported in our case studies, as well as technologies relevant to course content, such as online group games or simulations.

---

[2] The Command and General Staff College (CGSC) recently became the first defense service college to receive a waiver to move its education content from a constrained, defense-managed network to a dotcom environment (see Gould, 2013).

In our view, CGSS is an "early adopter," already ahead of the curve in experimenting with technology. We recommend staying on this course, but given the goals of AOC, the constraints students face, and the limitations of current ICTs for collaboration, we expect that a technological solution alone will not be sufficient to improve learning processes and outcomes significantly.

Recommendations for Course Evaluation

Future evaluations of intermediate level education courses should use a broader range of approaches. The course surveys seem to do a good job of capturing students' perceptions of learning effectiveness of satisfaction with the course. From our analysis of the entrance and exit surveys and the pilot test of the postgraduate survey, we have some recommendations for survey design that are described in Appendix B, along with a revised exit survey presented in Appendix C. However, as noted in Chapter Three, although students' assessments of their learning are often correlated with actual learning, survey responses are subjective. Future evaluations of AOC and other ILE courses should also analyze objective measures of learning, such as grades on assignments and tests. In addition, because many of the competencies addressed in AOC are abstract, it may be helpful to provide information to students to demonstrate their knowledge gain using a pretest-posttest approach. One approach is to "start at the end" by giving students a complex problem to solve at the beginning of the course to serve as a benchmark, then assigning the same or a similar problem at the end of the course, thus highlighting differences in their processes and performance over time.

Currently, CGSS does not have a good mechanism for assessing the perceptions of those who drop out of the course and their reasons for attrition. This omission is a key gap, given that the attrition rate is currently estimated at 25 percent. As a result of that high rate, current surveys likely overestimate satisfaction and the perceived learning effectiveness of the course. More important, the attrition rate significantly increases the cost of the course per graduate and keeps waiting lists unnecessarily long. Assessing reasons for attrition in more depth could lend additional urgency to the changes already suggested in this report or could lead to additional improvements in the course that could reduce the dropout rate (see Straus et al., 2011, for an example of an analysis of attrition from other Army courses). For example, if the factors that are most likely to lead to attrition can be identified, selection procedures or other mitigating strategies could be designed accordingly.

Using multiple methods and data sources in evaluation is important because it will provide information about different aspects of the course. Triangulating findings from multiple methods also can foster confidence in the reliability of the results. In addition to CGSS's ongoing evaluation efforts, it is important to assess any changes in course design and delivery.

Other strategies for evaluation include

- collecting data from commanders regarding graduates' job performance after completing AOC or measuring graduates' knowledge retention over time to assess the broader impact of the course
- having in-depth discussions with students and faculty through focus groups or interviews to obtain more detailed feedback about the learning experience and recommendations for improvement (although we note that students' responses to open-ended questions in the surveys provided a rich set of data that spoke to these issues)
- using web analytics to understand how students use online materials (e.g., amount of time spent on lessons)
- asking a set of independent SMEs to systematically observe class sessions (e.g., by joining DCO sessions) to offer suggestions for improving learning processes
- integrating findings from faculty surveys (currently conducted by CGSC) with data from these other sources.

Concluding Thoughts

The present study identified important options to consider when training complex material using group collaboration that is entirely distributed. Because AOC-BDL objectives and instructional methods support Army Learning Model goals and because the course has many positive features, this BL approach should be considered for other courses across the Army. In fact, findings in the study indicate that a blended model may a better alternative to ADL for the ILE Common Core and may also be useful to reduce classroom hours in TASS and resident venues. However, alternative approaches to collaboration are needed when course activities involve collaboration on complex material. CGSS's experience and continuous development and evaluation efforts put the school in a position to identify such improvements and inform the Army training community about use of BDL for education and training.

APPENDIX A

Intermediate-Level Education Advanced Operations Course Blocks, Learning Objectives, and Cognitive Levels of Learning

Table A.1
Overview of AOC-BDL Blocks, Hours, and Objectives

Block	Hours	Learning Goals, Learning Objectives, and Cognitive Level of Learning
Operations 100 Campaign Planning	66	Understand U.S. service doctrine as it relates to operational warfighting in a Joint, Interagency, Intergovernmental, Multi-National environment. Learning Objectives: • Produce a campaign plan. Level of learning: Synthesis • Analyze the considerations for deploying, employing, and sustaining forces at the operational level of war. Level: Analysis • Analyze the impact of culture and geography within diverse regional environments. Level: Analysis
Operations 200 Force Generation	34	Build, deploy, and maintain brigade level forces to support Army operational mission execution. Learning Objectives: • Manage the force generation process. Level: Synthesis • Integrate the functions of contracting, funding, and war-time host nation support into tactical execution. Level: Application

Table A.1—Continued

Block	Hours	Learning Goals, Learning Objectives, and Cognitive Level of Learning
Operations 300 Full Spectrum Operations	150	Execute brigade level missions in extended campaigns; understand the application of operational art in tactical planning; understand, visualize, and describe the operational environment; frame complex problems; and direct staffs. Learning Objective: • Evaluate the employment of Army tactical forces in full spectrum operations. Level: Evaluation
History 200	20	Apply the perspectives of military history to military problem solving. Learning Objectives: • Use historical context to inform professional military judgment. Level: Analysis • Explain the major factors that have shaped military innovation and institutional adaption. Level: Synthesis. • Communicate effectively. Level: Synthesis
History 300	16	Apply the perspectives of military history to military problem solving. Learning Objectives: • Use historical context to inform professional military judgment. Level: Analysis • Explain historical trends that shaped today's operational environment. Level: Analysis
Leadership 200	22	Understand the dynamics of organizational-level leadership and the competencies that make organizational leaders effective. Learning Objective: • Analyze the integration of leadership concepts into the execution of operational battle command. Level: Synthesis

NOTE: CGSS uses a version of Bloom's (1956; 1994) cognitive levels to describe course activities. CGSS's levels are: Knowledge-recall of specific information; comprehension-understanding the material; application-use of knowledge to solve problems; analysis-breaking material down into component parts to determine structures and relationships; synthesis-integrating parts into a new whole; evaluation-judging or weighing by building and using criteria and standards.

APPENDIX B

Psychometric Properties of Exit and Postgraduate Surveys

In this appendix, we present measurement characteristics for the exit and postgraduate surveys. We follow with recommendations for revisions for survey design for future evaluations.

Scale Reliability

With the exception of some questions about the quality of instruction and a few "miscellaneous" items, responses to most of the items rated on five-point scales in the exit survey were highly intercorrelated regardless of item topic. Thus, few scales or obvious groupings of items were evident based on patterns of students' responses. We grouped items by topic for ease in interpretation.

Table B.1 shows the item groupings and descriptive statistics for the exit survey.[1] Note that all items used five-point response options. Table B.2 shows the scales and descriptive statistics for the postgraduate survey. As shown in Table B.2., the number of response options varied for different questions in the postgraduate survey.

[1] Coefficient alpha is influenced by the number of items on a scale; thus, a scale with a few items will typically have a lower alpha than a scale with many items. Coefficient alpha is not applicable for items that do not use continuous scales (e.g., yes or no; rankings) or for topics for which there is a single item.

Table B.1
Exit Survey Scales and Descriptive Statistics

Factor	Topic	Scale or Item	Number of Items	Coeff. Alpha	Mean	Std. Dev.
Satisfaction	Virtual learning environment	Quality of instruction	6	0.87	4.32	0.69
		Value of peer feedback	1	n/a	4.04	0.91
	Global perceptions	Overall satisfaction	2	0.86	3.92	0.97
		Recommend AOC through DL to others	1	n/a	3.13	1.43
Learning effectiveness	History (CBI)		4	0.94	3.94	0.82
	Leadership (CBI)		4	0.88	3.76	0.84
	Operations		21	0.97	3.87	0. 67
	Critical field-grade competencies	Critical thinking	2	0.82	3.92	0.84
		Communication skills	2	0.87	3.58	0.93

Table B.2
Postgraduate Survey Scales and Descriptive Statistics

Factor	Scale or Item	Number of Items	Number of Response Options	Coeff. Alpha	Mean	Std. Dev.
Satisfaction	Overall satisfaction (includes "Recommend AOC through DL to others")	3	6	0. 93	4.31	1.37
Learning effectiveness	CBI	3	6	0.93	4.51	1.02
	Critical field-grade competencies	5	4	0.89	2.41	0.74
Collaborative processes	Interaction with instructor	2	6	0.75	4.48	1.17
	Collaboration with peers via DCO	1	6	na	4.06	1.30
	Ease of scheduling collaborative sessions with peers	1	6	na	3.03	1.24
	Team members pull their weight	1	6	na	3.70	1.46

Response Sets or Patterns

We also looked at student responses in terms of potential leniency bias and response fatigue. We examined patterns of responses to the 44 items in the exit survey that used five-point agree-disagree scales. Figure B.1 shows the average percentage of responses in each response option category for these items. The large percentages (76 percent) of "four" (agree) and "five" (strongly agree) ratings could indicate that students generally had favorable views of the course or that there was leniency in responding. These patterns are similar to those observed in end-of-course surveys of the ILE Common Core (Straus and Ward, 2011). There appears to be less leniency in the postgraduate survey, with 44 percent of responses in "agree" and "strongly agree" categories (15 items; six-point scales) (see Figure B.2).

Given the length of the exit survey, we also examined response patterns for possible automatic or careless responding. We had observed such patterns in our previous study of the Common Core (Straus and Ward, 2011), suggesting that students tended to "check the box" and give the same response across questions. Figure B.3 shows the percent-

Figure B.1
Average Percentage of Each Rating Across Items in Exit Survey

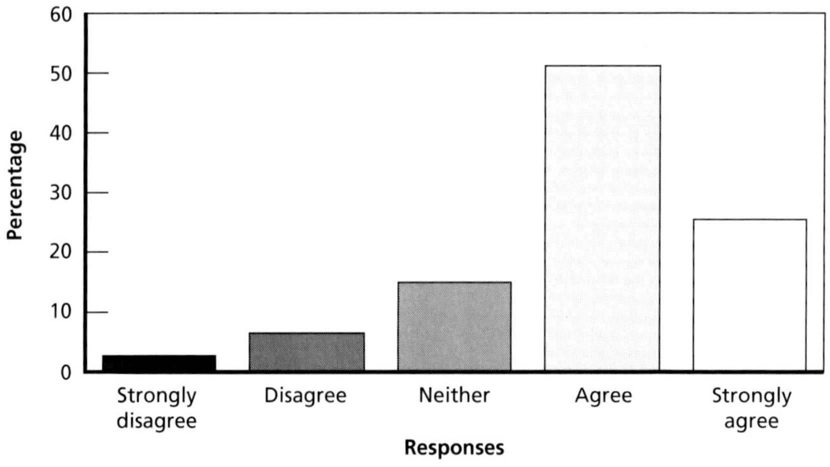

RAND *RR172-A-B.1*

Figure B.2
Average Percentage of Each Rating Across Items in Postgraduate Survey

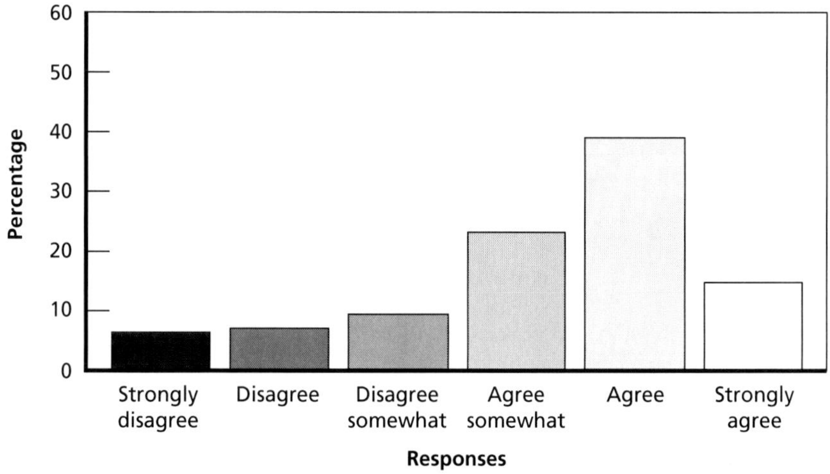

RAND *RR172-A-B.2*

Figure B.3
Percentage of Students Giving the Same Response Across Items in Advanced Operations Course and Common Core Surveys

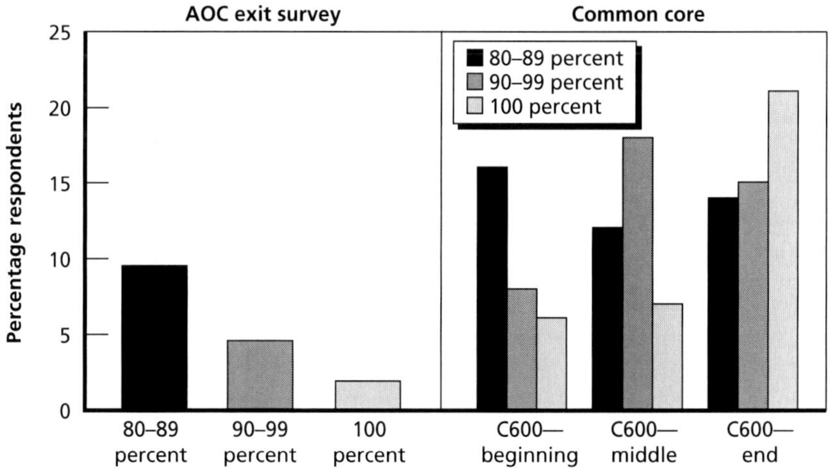

RAND *RR172-A-B.3*

age of students giving the same answer (e.g., all ones, all twos, etc.) across all items that used a five-point agree-disagree scale in the exit survey (chart on the left) and in a three of nine surveys administered in the resident Common Core course (chart on the right). Results are reported in terms of the percentage of survey participants that gave 80 to 89 percent, 90 to 99 percent, or 100 percent of their responses in each category. In contrast to the Common Core, results indicate minimal careless responding in AOC, suggesting that the survey is not burdensome. For example, less than 2 percent of AOC respondents gave the same answer to all questions (versus 6 to 21 percent in the Common Core), and less than 5 percent of AOC respondents gave the same answer to 90 to 99 percent of the questions (versus 8 to 18 percent in the Common Core). One exception, however, was responses to the 21 items about operations, as indicated by an extremely high coefficient alpha ($\alpha = 0.97$) (14 percent of students gave the same response to all these questions). Overall, results for AOC most likely differ from those in the Common Core because there was only one exit survey in AOC; in the Common Core, multiple surveys likely generated survey fatigue. Note that short survey or item response times would also be helpful in determining whether students are merely "checking the box," but these data were not available from the version of the LMS in use at the time.

Recommendations for Revisions to Survey Content and Format

Based on analysis of the entrance and exit surveys and our pilot test of the postgraduate survey, we have some recommendations for survey design and future research. Appendix C provides a revised exit survey.

Question Content

First, open-ended responses in the exit survey showed that the closed-ended or objective questions did not capture a number of important aspects influencing students' perceptions of the class. We recommend using closed-ended questions to assess collaboration and other input and process issues, as piloted in the postgraduate survey, because these responses can be analyzed more efficiently than responses to open-ended questions. While it is very useful to include open-ended survey questions, we suggest making them more focused.

Second, the exit survey consisted of a large number of detailed questions about substantive topics in the course, particularly about operations. As described above, students' ratings were very similar across all the operations topics, with no obvious subgroups of questions. We also question whether students recall how much they learned at this level of detail. Thus, we suggest devising questions about substantive topics at a more general level. Students can note needs for specific areas for improvement in their responses to an open-ended question about content (already included in the current version of the survey). The revised exit survey in Appendix C presents examples of general questions, but SMEs are needed to ensure that items are written to capture all key course topics.

Third, additional questions about student characteristics, many of which were included in the postgraduate survey, are needed to diagnose factors that influence learning processes and outcomes. Some of these questions can be refined further, e.g., by distinguishing work and family (which were included in a single item in the postgraduate survey). It would also be useful to include a question about officer rank. Moreover, it is essential to include questions about student characteristics and reactions to the course in the same survey if the intent is to examine the association of these inputs and outcomes while maintaining anonymous participation in the survey(s) (which we advocate to encourage candid responses). Some questions, such as readiness for AOC-BDL, are more appropriately included in an entrance survey; with anonymous participation, these questions can be used to identify needs for staff groups as a whole but cannot be linked to exit survey responses.

Question Format

The postgraduate survey included some questions that used four- or six-point scales with no midpoint, rather than five-point agree-disagree scales with a "neutral" midpoint. For questions about knowledge gain, in particular, response options were made more specific by asking for the degree of improvement in terms of none, a small amount, moderate, or substantial. These types of options seem to provide more unequivocal feedback from students. However, additional research is needed to determine whether odd or even numbers of response options are preferable and what response option labels are most informative. Results in the research literature regarding the optimal number of response options are mixed, as noted in reviews by Chang (1994) and Cox (1980). For example, some studies have found that internal-consistency reliability is not influenced by the number of response options, while other studies have found evidence that either three-, five-, or seven-point scales are superior or that the optimal number depends on homogeneity of item content. Still others have found that odd numbers of options cause response sets or patterns (e.g., central tendency, or the tendency to select the midpoint of the scale—although responses in ILE surveys tend to show leniency rather than central tendency responses). In addition to internal-consistency reliability, other measurement characteristics to consider include the degree to which responses discriminate among respondents with different underlying attitudes and the amount of information provided by responses. Moreover, to conduct a robust test of alternative response options, such methods as administering the same questions with different scales to a large sample of individuals are needed.

Also note that the use of different response options (true-or-false questions, five-point Likert-type scales, four-point Likert-type scales) for similar questions (such as questions about readiness for the course in the entrance survey) precluded combining responses to create scales or groups of items, which are more reliable than single items. In the future, using the same set of response options (e.g., four- or six-point agree-disagree scales) for similar questions would facilitate analysis.

Finally, to build on the CGSS's continuous quality improvement efforts, we recommend piloting the revised survey to test new questions and response option formats. In keeping with these efforts, we suggest modifying the items over time as needed. For example, if a particular technical issue is resolved, questions about that issue can be eliminated; likewise, if changes are made to the course, questions should be added to assess reactions to the change.

APPENDIX C

Proposed Exit Survey Questions

The proposed items and response options in Tables C.1 through C.4 are based on the current course design and technologies; revisions to item content or response options will be needed as the course changes over time. Where possible, it is preferable to provide response options or choices rather than allowing students to fill in the blank. Fixed responses will limit the manner in which students provide the information, thereby facilitating analysis.

Table C.1
Proposed Revisions to Exit Survey—Student Background Characteristics

Item	Response Options
Demographic characteristics and experience	
What is your component?	AC, RC
What is your rank?	Major, Lieutenant Colonel
What is your career field?	I am Army, but have not yet received a Career Field Designation; Maneuver, Fires, and Effects; Operations Support; Force Sustainment; Health Services; other
At what echelon or equivalent echelon are you most likely to serve immediately after graduating from AOC?	Brigade, division, corps
In what type of organization are you most likely to serve immediately after graduation from AOC?	Army operational unit, Army generating force organization, joint, interagency, other
What is your marital status?	Single, married, single with children, married with children
What is your employment status?	Work full time, work part time, unemployed
When did you complete AOC?	2012, 2011, 2010, 2009, I don't remember
In what month did you complete AOC?	JAN–DEC, I don't remember
Where were you located when you took AOC?	CONUS, OCONUS, both
Did you PCS, TCS, go on extended TDY, move, or deploy during AOC?	Yes, no, do not remember
Approximately how many hours per week did you spend working on AOC?	1–4, 5–8, 9–12, 13–16, 17–20, more than 20 hours
Did you complete the majority of the AOC content on duty time/paid status or on your own time?	Paid time, own time, equal amounts of duty time and my own time

Table C.1—Continued

Item	Response Options
Why did you take AOC? (Rank order)	Improve my professionalism or ability to perform in current and expected assignment; meet requirements or enhance my chances for promotion; other (fill in the blank)
In what year did you complete the ILE Common Core?	e.g., 2012, 2011, 2010, 2009, I don't remember
In what venue(s) did you take the ILE Common Core?	Resident at Ft. Leavenworth, resident at a satellite location, entirely ADL, entirely TASS, I switched from TASS to all ADL or from all ADL to TASS
Technology reliability; obstacles to participation	
To what extent did you have technical difficulties with CBI/flash lessons?	Not at all, somewhat, a great extent
To what extent did the following interfere with your ability to work on the course: Work commitments Family commitments Access to technical support Access to a reliable computer Access to reliable Internet access	Not at all, somewhat, a great extent

Table C.2
Proposed Revisions to Exit Survey—Learning Effectiveness

Item	Response Options
Overall perceptions	
ILE's Core Purpose (CGSC Circular 350-1) is "to prepare field grade officers with a warrior ethos and war fighting focus for leadership positions in Army, Joint, Multinational, and Interagency organizations executing full spectrum operations." Did CGSC achieve the ILE Core Purpose during your ILE experience?	Yes, somewhat, no
If answered "No or Somewhat" in the previous question, what part of the ILE Core Purpose was not achieved during your ILE experience?	Open-ended
Did ILE prepare you to operate as a field-grade commander and staff officer in full-spectrum...(Select all the apply)	Army, joint, multinational, interagency
Critical field-grade skills	
To what degree has AOC improved your: Ability to solve complex problems Written communication skills Oral communication skills Organizational leadership skills Ability to conduct MDMP	Not at all A small amount A moderate amount A substantial amount
Substantive topics (history, leadership, operations)[a]	
Course meaningfully increased:	Five- or six-point agree-disagree scales
My ability to use historical lessons learned as a tool when making military decisions	
My understanding of land component command operations	
My knowledge of the joint operational planning process	
My understanding of the Army change management process	

Table C.2—Continued

Item	Response Options
What wasn't taught (if anything) in AOC, that should have been taught to better prepare you for the positions you have had or anticipate having?	Open-ended
What was taught (if anything) that hasn't been useful in preparing you for the positions you have or anticipate to have?	Open-ended
CBI	
Computer-based instruction (CBI)/flash lessons meaningfully improved my knowledge of Military operations Military history Leadership	Five- or six-point agree-disagree scales
Readings and assignments	Five- or six-point agree-disagree scales
Course readings improved my knowledge of course topics	
Individual assignments meaningfully contributed to my knowledge of course topics	
Group assignments meaningful contributed to my knowledge about course topics	

[a] Rather than asking many detailed questions about course topics, we suggest asking fewer, more general questions. We present these items as examples of questions written at a general level; however, SMEs are needed to write questions that capture the range of topics covered in the course.

Table C.3
Proposed Revisions to Exit Survey—Learning Processes

Item	Response Options
Collaboration and technology	
DCO sessions with the instructor meaningfully contributed to achieving AOC's learning objectives	Five- or six-point agree-disagree scales
Online threaded discussions meaningfully contributed to achieving AOC's learning objectives	
Group interaction meaningfully contributed to achieving the objectives of the course	
I learned a great deal from my peers in the class	
Members of my group(s) pulled their weight	
DCO was effective for group collaboration	
My group(s) had difficulties finding time to schedule collaborative sessions	
Indicate how the extent to which you agree that each of the following methods was for effective for group collaboration DCO sessions Blackboard filesharing AKO filesharing Email Online chat Telephone conversations Videoconferencing, such as Skype Social media (e.g., Facebook, MilBook, blogs, wikis) Face-to-face interaction Other	Five- or six-point agree-disagree scales; did not use
If you selected "Other" to the question above, list the other method(s) your group used to collaborate during AOC	Open-ended

Table C.3—Continued

Item	Response Options
I received sufficient training on how to use collaborative technologies for the course	Five- or six-point agree-disagree scales
DCO was easy to use	Five- or six-point agree-disagree scales
Blackboard was easy to use	Five- or six-point agree-disagree scales
Please describe any additional comments about the effectiveness of the methods your group(s) used to collaborate or recommendations to make collaboration more effective.	Open-ended

Table C.4
Proposed Revisions to Exit Survey—Student Satisfaction

Item	Response options
Virtual classroom environment	
The instructor provided adequate interaction opportunities	Five- or six-point agree-disagree scales
The instructor provided relevant feedback	
I received timely feedback on assignments	
The instructor encouraged critical thinking	
Overall satisfaction	
Overall, I was satisfied with what I learned in AOC	Five- or six-point agree-disagree scales
The amount of learning I achieved in the course was worth the effort required	
I would recommend AOC via distributed learning to others	
If you answered "disagree somewhat, disagree, or strongly disagree" to the question above, what are the main reasons that you would not recommend the course to others?	Open-ended
How would you compare the instructional methods in AOC with the method of delivery you experienced for the Common Core?	Much worse, somewhat worse, about the same, somewhat better, much better

APPENDIX D

Case Study Interview Questions

Interviews were conducted in person or by phone between March and August 2012. We followed a semistructured interview protocol. Interviews with program or center directors and staff were designed to get a sense of institutional supports for DL programs, such as instructional designers and professional development for faculty new to DL instruction. For interviews with instructors, the goal was to solicit information about program or course structure, content, learning goals, resources, students (including quantity and characteristics), instructors, evaluations, and instructional modality and media mix.

Questions for Program or Center Directors and Staff

1. What is your professional background? How long have you been directing this program/center?
2. Can you describe the history of the program (e.g., when it was established, motivation for establishing it, start-up resources needed)?
3. What is the current status of the program (number and type of courses/certifications, students, staff, operating resources, effectiveness, etc.)?
4. What types of instructional support does the program/center offer instructors?

5. (If the interview included instructional designers) What kinds of professional backgrounds do your instructional designers have, and how do they work with instructors to design courses?
6. Does your program/center offer professional development for instructors? If so, what kind of development is offered?
7. What successes and challenges has the program experienced?
8. Are there plans to change the program, including plans for expansion or contraction?

Questions for Instructors

1. What is your professional background (including instructional experience)?
2. What online courses are you currently teaching or have most recently taught?
3. Can you describe the course(s)? Please provide information about the following:
   - goals, content, and structure
   - instructional media and modalities
   - student characteristics
   - assignments and grading criteria
   - resources needed to maintain the course(s).
4. Briefly describe the history of each course, including
   - when it was established and why
   - learning models/theories that underlay the course and instructional design
   - your role (if any) in establishing the course.
5. Is there an in-residence version of this course? If so, can you briefly describe it?
   - Can students self-select into either venue (in residence or online)?
   - How much overlap is there in instructional design between the in-residence and online versions of the course?
6. How do you measure the effectiveness of the course? What have been the results?

7. What successes and challenges have you experienced in (developing and) teaching this course?
8. What plans, if any, are there to modify the online course in substantive ways (e.g., introduce a new type of instructional medium, improve an existing medium)?

References

Adelson, Jill L., and D. Betsy McCoach, "The Mathematical Attitudes of Elementary Students: The Effects of a 4-Point or 5-Point Likert-Type Scale," *Educational and Psychological Measurement*, Vol. 70, No. 5, October 2010, pp. 796–807.

Al-Busaidi, Kamla Ali, and Hafedh Al-Shihi, "Key Factors to Instructors' Satisfaction of Learning Management Systems in Blended Learning," *Journal of Computing in Higher Education*, 2012, pp. 1–22.

Alberts, David S., and Richard E. Hayes, "Power to the Edge: Command, Control in the Information Age," *Command and Control Research Program*, 2003.

Allen, I. Elaine, and Jeff Seaman, *Going the Distance: Online Education in the United States*, San Francisco: Babson Survey Research Group and Quahog Research Group, LLC, 2011.

Alliger, George M., Scott I. Tannenbaum, Winston Bennett Jr., Holly Traver, and Allison Shotland, "A Meta-Analysis of the Relations Among Training Criteria," *Personnel Psychology*, Vol. 50, No. 2, 1997, pp. 341–358.

Alonso, Fernando, Daniel Manrique, and Jose M. Vines, "A Moderate Constructivist e-Learning Instructional Model Evaluated on Computer Specialists," *Computers & Education*, Vol. 53, No. 1, August 2009, pp. 57–65.

Arbaugh, J. B., "Does the Community of Inquiry Framework Predict Outcomes in Online MBA Courses?" *International Review of Research in Open and Distance Learning*, Vol. 9, No. 2, June 2008, pp. 1–21.

Armstrong, David J., and Paul Cole, "Managing Distances and Differences in Geographically Distributed Work Groups," in Pamela J. Hinds and Sara Kiesler, eds., *Distributed Work*, Cambridge, Mass.: MIT Press, 2002, pp. 167–186.

Axtell, Carolyn M., Steven J. Fleck, and Nick Turner, "Virtual Teams: Collaborating Across Distance," *International Review of Industrial and Organizational Psychology*, Vol. 19, 2004, pp. 205–248.

Baltes, Boris B., Marcus W. Dickson, Michael P. Sherman, Cara C. Bauer, and Jacqueline S. LaGanke, "Computer-Mediated Communication and Group Decision Making: A Meta-Analysis," *Organizational Behavior and Human Decision Processes*, Vol. 87, No. 1, 2002, pp. 156–179.

Benbunan-Fich, Raquel, Starr Roxanne Hiltz, and Linda Harasim, "The Online Interaction Learning Model: An Integrated Theoretical Framework for Learning Networks," in Starr Roxanne Hiltz and Ricki Goldman, eds., *Learning Together Online: Research on Asynchronous Learning Networks*, Mahwah, N.J.: Lawrence Erlbaum, 2005, pp. 19–37.

Bernard, Robert M., Philip C. Abrami, Yiping Lou, Evgueni Borokhovski, Anne Wade, Lori Wozney, Peter A. Wallet, Manon Fiset, and Binru Huang, "How Does Distance Education Compare with Classroom Instruction? A Meta-Analysis of the Empirical Literature," *Review of Educational Research*, Vol. 74, No. 3, 2004, pp. 379–439.

Bersin, Josh, Kim Lamoureux, David Mallon, Stacey Harris, Stacia Garr, Laci (Barb) Loew, and Steve Goldberg, *Learning Leaders 2012: Lessons from the Best,* Oakland, Calif.: Bersin & Associates, February 2012. As of September 19, 2012: http://marketing.bersin.com/2012LearningLeaders.html

Bisson, Barry, Edward Leach, Timothy Little, Robert Richards, Brian Veitch, and Karin Zunkel, "A Case Study in Blended Learning: Leveraging Technology in Entrepreneurship Education," in John Bourne and Janet C. Moore, eds., *Elements of Quality in Online Education: Engaging Communities*, Needham, Mass.: Sloan-C, 2005, pp. 41–54.

Bloom, Benjamin S., *Taxonomy of Educational Objectives, Handbook I: Cognitive Domain*, New York: David McKay Company, 1956.

———, "Reflections on the Development and Use of the Taxonomy," in Lorin W. Anderson and Lauren A. Sosniak, eds., *Bloom's Taxonomy: A Forty-Year Retrospective*, Chicago: University of Chicago Press, 1994.

Bonk, Curtis J., and Charles R. Graham, *The Handbook of Blended Learning: Global Perspectives, Local Designs*, San Francisco: Pfeiffer, 2006.

Bonk, Curtis J., K. J. Kim, and T. Zeng, "Future Directions of Blended Learning in Higher Education and Workplace Learning Settings," in Curtis J. Bonk and Charles R. Graham, eds., *Handbook of Blended Learning: Global Perspectives, Local Designs*, San Francisco: Pfeiffer, 2006, pp. 550–567.

Bonk, Curtis J., Tatana M. Olson, Robert A. Wisher, and Kara L. Orvis, "Learning from Focus Groups: An Examination of Blended Learning," *The Journal of Distance Education*, Vol. 17, No. 3, 2002, pp. 97–118.

Brandon Hall Group, "Winners of the 2011 Brandon Hall Excellence in Learning Awards," web page, 2012. As of May 8, 2013: http://brandonhall.com/excellence-learning.php?year=2011

CGSS—*See* Command and General Staff School.

Chang, Lei, "A Psychometric Evaluation of 4-Point and 6-Point Likert-Type Scales in Relation to Reliability and Validity," *Applied Psychological Measurement*, Vol. 18, No. 3, 1994, pp. 205–215.

Clark, Ruth C., and Richard E. Mayer, *E-Learning and the Science of Instruction: Proven Guidelines for Consumers and Designers of Multimedia Learning*, San Francisco: Pfeiffer, 2011.

Colazo, Jorge A., "Exploring the Association Between Temporal Dispersion and Virtual Team Performance," *Proceedings of the 43rd Hawaii International Conference on System Sciences*, Washington, D.C.: IEEE Computer Society, 2010, pp. 1–7.

Command and General Staff School, "The CGSC Experiential Learning Model," 2005.

———, "Intermediate Level Education (ILE) Common Core Syllabus," December 2009.

———, "Advanced Operations Course (AOC) Syllabus," December 2010.

———, "Information Paper Intermediate Level Education (ILE)," September 23, 2011.

Conole, Gráinne, and Panagiota Alevizou, *A Literature Review of the Use of Web 2.0 Tools in Higher Education*, Milton Keynes, U.K.: The Open University, 2010.

Cox, Eli P., "The Optimal Number of Response Alternatives for a Scale: A Review," *Journal of Marketing Research*, 1980, pp. 407–422.

Cramton, Catherine D., "The Mutual Knowledge Problem and Its Consequences for Dispersed Collaboration," *Organization Science*, Vol. 12, No. 3, 2001, pp. 346–371.

Cramton, Catherine D., Kara L. Orvis, and Jeanne M. Wilson, "Situation Invisibility and Attribution in Distributed Collaborations," *Journal of Management*, Vol. 33, No. 4, 2007, pp. 525–546.

Department of the Army, *Officer Professional Development and Career Management*, DA Pamphlet 600-3, February 2010.

DoD—*See* U.S. Department of Defense.

Francescato, Donata, Minou Mebane, Rita Porcelli, Carlo Attanasio, and Marcella Pulino, "Developing Professional Skills and Social Capital Through Computer Supported Collaborative Learning in University Contexts," *International Journal of Human-Computer Studies*, Vol. 65, No. 2, February 2007, pp. 140–152.

Galegher, Jolene, and Robert E. Kraut, "Computer-Mediated Communication and Collaborative Writing: Media Influence and Adaptation to Communication Constraints," *Proceedings of the Conference on Computer Supported Cooperative Work (CSCW)* '92, New York: ACM Press, 1992, pp. 155–162.

Gould, Joe, "Army's Learning Cloud Means Accessible Class Materials," *Defense News*, April 22, 2013. As of April 23, 2013: http://www.defensenews.com/article/20130422/TSJ01/304220019/Army-s-learning-cloud-means-accessible-class-materials?odyssey=mod|newswell|text|FRONTPAGE|p

Graham, Charles R., "Blended Learning Systems: Definitions, Current Trends, and Future Directions," in Curtis J. Bonk and Charles R. Graham, *The Handbook of Blended Learning Global Perspectives, Local Designs*, San Francisco: Pfeiffer, 2006, pp. 3–21.

Graham, Charles R., S. Allen, and D. Ure, *Blended Learning: A Review of the Literature*, unpublished manuscript, Provo, Utah: Brigham Young University, 2003.

Griffith, Terri L., and Margaret A. Neale, "Information Processing in Traditional, Hybrid, and Virtual Teams: From Nascent Knowledge to Transactive Memory," *Research in Organizational Behavior*, Vol. 23, 2001, pp. 379–421.

Hinds, Pamela J., and Suzanne P. Weisband, "Knowledge Sharing and Shared Understanding in Virtual Teams," in Cristina B. Gibson and Susan G. Cohen, eds., *Virtual Teams That Work: Creating Conditions for Virtual Teams Effectiveness*, San Francisco: Jossey-Bass, 2003, pp. 21–36.

Hollingshead, Andrea B., Joseph E. McGrath, and Kathleen M. O'Connor, "Group Task Performance and Communication Technology: A Longitudinal Study of Computer-Mediated Versus Face-to-Face Work Groups," *Small Group Research*, Vol. 24, No. 3, 1993, pp. 307–333.

Hu, Paul J. H., Theodore H. K. Clark, and Will W. Ma, "Examining Technology Acceptance by School Teachers: A Longitudinal Study," *Information & Management*, Vol. 41, No. 2, 2003, pp. 227–241.

Jones, Norah, Haydn Blackey, Karen Fitzgibbon, and Esyin Chew, "Get Out of MySpace!" *Computers & Education*, Vol. 54, No. 3, 2010, pp. 776–782.

Kayser, Thomas A., *Mining Group Gold: How to Cash in on the Collaborative Brain Power of a Team for Innovation and Results*, New York: McGraw-Hill, 2010.

Kiesler, Sarah, David Zubrow, Anne Marie Moses, and Valerie Geller, "Affect in Computer-Mediated Communication: An Experiment in Synchronous Terminal-to-Terminal Discussion," *Human-Computer Interaction*, Vol. 1, No. 1, 1985, pp. 77–104.

Kolb, David A., *Experiential Learning: Experience as the Source of Learning and Development*, Englewood Cliffs, N.J.: Prentice-Hall, 1984.

Kraut, Robert E., Robert S. Fish, Robert W. Root, and Barbara L. Chalfonte, "Informal Communication in Organizations: Form, Function, and Technology," in Stuart Oskamp and Shirlynn Spacapan, eds., *Human Reactions to Technology: The Claremont Symposium on Applied Social Psychology*, Beverly Hills, Calif.: Sage Publications, 1990, pp. 145–199.

Kraut, Robert E., Susan R. Fussell, Susan E. Brennan, and Jane Siegel, "Understanding Effects of Proximity on Collaboration: Implications for Technologies to Support Remote Collaborative Work," in Pamela J. Hinds and Sara Kiesler, eds., *Distributed Work*, Cambridge, Mass.: MIT Press, 2002, pp. 137–162.

Kvavik, Robert B., and Judith B. Caruso, *ECAR Study of Students and Information Technology, 2005: Convenience, Connection, Control, and Learning*, Boulder, Colo.: EDUCAUSE Center for Applied Research, Vol. 6, 2005.

Lion, Robert W., and Gary Stark, "A Glance at Institutional Support for Faculty Teaching in an Online Learning Environment," *Educause Quarterly,* Vol. 33, No. 3, September 2010. As of December 10, 2012:
http://www.educause.edu/ero/article/
glance-institutional-support-faculty-teaching-online-learning-environment

Lockee, Barbara B., and Michelle A. Reece, "Instructional Technology Graduate Programs in Support of Corporate E-Learning," in John Bourne and Janet C. Moore, eds., *Elements of Quality in Online Education: Engaging Communities*, Needham, Mass.: Sloan-C, 2005, pp. 117–127.

Ma, Will W-K, Robert Andersson, and Karl-Oskar Streith, "Examining User Acceptance of Computer Technology: An Empirical Study of Student Teachers," *Journal of Computer Assisted Learning*, Vol. 21, No. 6, 2005, pp. 387–395.

Means, Barbara, Yukie Toyama, Robert Murphy, Marianne Bakia, and Karla Jones, *Evaluation of Evidence-Based Practices in Online Learning: A Meta-Analysis and Review of Online Learning Studies*, Washington, D.C.: U.S. Department of Education, Office of Planning, Evaluation, and Policy Development, 2009.

Miller, Kelly, "Wholly Online Learning in Environmental Science," *International Journal of Learning,* Vol. 13, No. 10, 2007, pp. 95–103.

Moore, Geoffrey, *Crossing the Chasm: Marketing and Selling High-Tech Products to Mainstream Customers*, New York: Harper Business Essentials, 2002.

Moore, Michael G., "Editorial: Three Types of Interaction," *American Journal of Distance Education*, Vol. 3, 1989, pp. 1–7.

Nonaka, Ikujiro, "A Dynamic Theory of Organizational Knowledge Creation," *Organization Science*, Vol. 5, No. 1, 1994, pp. 14–37.

O'Neill, Susan, Murray Scott, and Kieran Conboy, "A Delphi Study on Collaborative Learning in Distance Education: The Faculty Perspective," *British Journal of Educational Technology*, Vol. 42, No. 6, November 2011, pp. 939–949.

Park, Yun J., and Curtis J. Bonk, "Is Online Life a Breeze? A Case Study for Promoting Synchronous Learning in a Blended Graduate Course," *MERLOT Journal of Online Learning and Teaching*, Vol. 3, No. 3, 2007a, pp. 307–323.

———, "Synchronous Learning Experiences: Distance and Residential Learners' Perspectives in a Blended Graduate Course," *Journal of Interactive Online Learning*, Vol. 6, No. 3, 2007b, pp. 245–264.

Peters, Vanessa L., and Jim Hewitt, "An Investigation of Student Practices in Asynchronous Computer Conferencing Courses," *Computers & Education*, Vol. 54, No. 4, May, 2010, pp. 951–961.

Phipps, Ronald A., and Jamie P. Merisotis, *What's the Difference? A Review of Contemporary Research on the Effectiveness of Distance Learning in Higher Education*, Washington, D.C.: Institute for Higher Education Policy, 1999.

Quality Matters Program, "Quality Matters Rubric Standards 2011–2013 Edition with Assigned Point Values," MarylandOnline, Inc., 2011. As of September 20, 2012:
http://www.qmprogram.org/files/QM_Standards_2011-2013.pdf

Schneckenberg, Dirk, "Overcoming Barriers for eLearning in Universities—Porfolio Models for eCompetence Development of Faculty," *British Journal of Educational Technology*, Vol. 41, No. 6, 2010, pp. 979–991.

Shanley, Michael G., Matthew W. Lewis, Susan G. Straus, Jeff Rothenberg, and Lindsay Daugherty, *The Prospects for Increasing the Reuse of Digital Training Content*, Santa Monica, Calif.: RAND Corporation, MG-732-OSD, 2009. As of January 24, 2013:
http://www.rand.org/pubs/monographs/MG732.html

Sitzmann, Traci, Kenneth G. Brown, Wendy J. Casper, Katherine Ely, and Ryan D. Zimmerman, "A Review and Meta-Analysis of the Nomological Network of Trainee Reactions," *Journal of Applied Psychology*, Vol. 93, No. 2, 2008, pp. 280–295.

Sitzmann, Traci, Kurt Kraiger, David Stewart, and Robert Wisher, "The Comparative Effectiveness of Web-Based and Classroom Instruction: A Meta-Analysis," *Personnel Psychology*, Vol. 59, No. 3, 2006, pp. 623–664.

Sloan Consortium, "The Five Pillars," web page, 2012. As of January 24, 2013:
http://sloanconsortium.org/5pillars

So, Hyo-Jeong, and Curtis J. Bonk, "Examining the Roles of Blended Learning Approaches in Computer-Supported Collaborative Learning (CSCL) Environments: A Delphi Study," *Educational Technology & Society*, Vol. 13, No. 3, July 2010, pp. 189–200.

Straus, Susan G., "Technology, Group Process, and Group Outcomes: Testing the Connections in Computer-Mediated and Face-to-Face Groups," *Human-Computer Interaction*, Vol. 12, No. 3, 1997, pp. 227–266.

Straus, Susan G., and Joseph E. McGrath, "Does the Medium Matter? The Interaction of Task Type and Technology on Group Performance and Member Reactions," *Journal of Applied Psychology*, Vol. 79, No. 1, 1994, p. 87.

Straus, Susan G., Jolene Galegher, Michael Shanley, and Joy S. Moini, *Improving the Effectiveness of Distributed Learning: A Research and Policy Agenda*, Santa Monica, Calif.: RAND Corporation, OP-156-A, 2006. As of January 24, 2012: http://www.rand.org/pubs/occasional_papers/OP156.html

Straus, Susan G., and Fernando Olivera, "Knowledge Acquisition in Virtual Teams," in Terri Griffith, ed., *Research on Managing Groups and Teams*, Vol. 3, JAI Press, 2000, pp. 257–282.

Straus, Susan G., Michael G. Shanley, Douglas Yeung, James Rothenberg, Elizabeth D. Steiner, and Kristin J. Leuschner, *New Tools and Metrics for Evaluating Army Distributed Learning*, Santa Monica, Calif.: RAND Corporation, MG-1072-A, 2011. As of January 24, 2012:
http://www.rand.org/pubs/monographs/MG1072.html

Straus, Susan G., and Daniel Ward, "Evaluating Delivery Venues for Teaching Critical Thinking Skills," presented at the Tenth Annual Army DL Workshop, Newport News, Va., June 2011.

Tallent-Runnels, Mary K., Julie A. Thomas, William Y. Lan, Sandi Cooper, Terence C. Ahern, Shana M. Shaw, and Xiaoming Liu, "Teaching Courses Online: A Review of the Research," *Review of Educational Research*, Vol. 76, No. 1, 2006, pp. 93–135.

Theroux, James, and Clare Kilbane, "The Real-Time Case Method: The Internet Creates the Potential for New Pedagogy," in John Bourne and Janet C. Moore, eds., *Elements of Quality in Online Education: Engaging Communities*, Needham, Mass.: Sloan-C, 2005, pp. 31–40.

Tucker, Jennifer S., David H. McGilvray, Bruce C. Leibrecht, Christopher B. Strauss, Andy Perrault, and Amanda N. Gesselman, *Training Digital Skills In Distributed Classroom Environments: A Blended Learning Approach*, Arlington, Va.: U.S. Army Research Institute for the Behavioral and Social Sciences, Research Report 1893, 2010.

U.S. Army Training and Doctrine Command, *The U.S. Army Learning Concept for 2015*, PAM 525-8-2, 2011.

U.S. Combined Arms Center, *Leader Development and Education (LD&E)/US Army Command and General Staff College Faculty and Staff Development Programs*, Bulletin No. 907, 2010.

U.S. Department of Defense (DoD), *Department of Defense Handbook: Development of Interactive Multimedia Instruction (IMI) (Part 3 of 5 Parts)*, 1999.

Venkatesh, Viswanath, Michael G. Morris, Gordon B. Davis, and Fred D. Davis, "User Acceptance of Information Technology: Toward a Unified View," *MIS Quarterly*, Vol. 27, No. 3, 2003, pp. 425–478.

Walther, Joseph B., "Impression Development in Computer-Mediated Interaction," *Western Journal of Communication*, Vol. 57, No. 4, 1993, pp. 381–398.

Webb, Noreen M., "Testing a Theoretical Model of Student Interaction and Learning in Small Groups," in Rachel Hertz-Lazarowitz and Norman Miller, eds., *Interaction in Cooperative Groups: The Theoretical Anatomy of Group Learning*, New York: Cambridge University Press, 1992.

Wilson, Jeanne M., Susan G. Straus, and William J. McEvily, "All in Due Time: The Development of Trust in Computer-Mediated and Face-to-Face Teams," *Organizational Behavior and Human Decision Processes*, Vol. 99, No. 1, 2006, pp. 16–33.

Wisher, Robert A., "ADL: Foundations for Global E-Learning Interoperability," *Proceedings of eLearning and Software for Education Conference*, No. 1, 2011, pp. 33–41,

Wisher, Robert A., Matthew V. Champagne, Jennifer L. Pawluk, Angela Eaton, and David M. Thornton, *Training Through Distance Learning: An Assessment of Research Findings*, Alexandria, Va.: U.S. Army Research Institute for Behavioral and Social Sciences, 1999.